Build Your Own PC
Third Edition

Build Your Own PC
Third Edition

Morris Rosenthal

McGraw-Hill/Osborne

New York Chicago San Francisco Lisbon London Madrid Mexico City
Milan New Delhi San Juan Seoul Singapore Sydney Toronto

McGraw-Hill/Osborne
2600 Tenth Street
Berkeley, California 94710
U.S.A.

To arrange bulk purchase discounts for sales promotions, premiums, or fund-raisers, please contact McGraw-Hill/Osborne at the above address. For information on translations or book distributors outside the U.S.A., please see the International Contact Information page immediately following the index of this book.

Build Your Own PC, Third Edition

34567890 QPD QPD 0198765432

ISBN 0-07-219558-4

Publisher
  Brandon A. Nordin

Vice President & Associate Publisher
  Scott Rogers

Acquisitions Editor
  Marjorie McAneny

Project Editor
  Pamela Woolf

Acquisitions Coordinator
  Emma Acker

Technical Editor
  Karen Weinstein

Copy Editor
  Rachel Lopez

Indexer
  Karin Arrigoni

Computer Designers
  Melinda Moore Lytle, Tara A. Davis, Jean Butterfield

Illustrators
  Michael Mueller, Lyssa Wald

Cover Design
  Tisa Lerner

This book was composed with Corel VENTURA™ Publisher.

Contents

Introduction

The purpose of this book is to get you building your own PC. The approach is to illustrate the process with hundreds of step-by-step photographs accompanied by specific assembly instructions. There are three complete build stories in this book, from a powerful system that can rival any server or workstation to a least cost, small footprint PC. Some of the steps appear almost identical from system to system, but we vary the camera angles and the order in which the steps are done to cover as many bases as possible. The point is that we aren't going to leave out a crucial step or show you how to do something wrong just for the sake of variety.

Chapter 1 contains a review of all the basic PC parts and their functions. Chapter 2 moves on to the subject of shopping for parts and understanding the dollars versus performance tradeoff. Chapter 3 presents information about handling and assembling PC parts and some common pitfalls you can avoid. In Chapter 4 we assemble a Pentium 4 system in a tower case with options for advanced storage solutions. Chapter 5 is an Athlon/Duron build in a midtower case configured like a typical home PC. The final build (Chapter 6) is an extremely cost-effective Pentium III/Celeron assembled in a minitower case. Chapter 7 looks at a typical Windows XP installation. And, Chapter 8 consists of troubleshooting checklists in case you encounter problems getting your new PC running.

One of the hardest choices for the author of a PC book is whether to include pricing information, which changes faster than ink dries. While we include pricing for basic parts that will result in a complete PC with a price tag under $400 to high-performance parts that will add up to a system costing thousands of dollars, these amounts are entirely dependant on current market conditions. We do not offer competitive reviews or present "roundups" of competing components. This is the domain of PC magazines and Web sites, some of which offer daily updates. This book does supply you with the vocabulary and examples needed to shop for ultra–high-performance parts, but its primary focus is on the practical considerations of purchasing and assembling home PCs.

The toughest decision for a new PC builder is how much to spend on parts. If you're on a limited budget, be thankful, because once you know how much you're going to spend, the rest is easy. Until you make the dollars decision, shopping will be a nightmare. For every component you consider, there will be a faster one or a higher capacity unit available for just another $20 or $50. The next performance level can be reached for $75 or $100 and so on, until you reach the latest and greatest component in every category and exceed the limit on your credit card. Three months later you'll open the newspaper or be surfing the Web and see an ad for a PC with exactly the same capabilities as yours, but it will already be $500 less than the one you put together. Don't spend more now in the hopes of keeping up with the future. Wait for the future and upgrade. Once you've built your own PC, you'll see how easily and cost-effectively you can upgrade if the need arises.

Chapter 1

First-time Builders

This chapter is written for first-time PC builders who have limited experience with PC hardware. Our main focus here will be to supply you with the necessary tools to move on to the job of selecting and purchasing components. The main tool needed for this task is a genuine understanding of the vocabulary of PCs. Keep in mind that learning a new vocabulary is like learning a foreign language. You only need to memorize a couple words to ask a question, but you need a degree of fluency to understand the answer. Feel free to skim or skip over any terms or parts you are already comfortable with. However, even if you've been using a PC longer than a microwave oven, you might find that you know less about what goes on inside than you thought. After all, how many people know that a microwave oven uses a 2.2 GHz (gigahertz) magnetron tube to heat the food, or why?

Speaking of gigahertz, now is a good a time as any to get the most basic part of PC vocabulary out of the way, the units of measure. Almost all PC components will have one or more units attached to them to describe storage capacity (bytes), speed (hertz, seconds), transfer rate (bits or bytes per second), power (watts), and visual properties (dots per inch, dot size). Most of these units are expressed in quantities of thousands, millions and billions, or the reciprocal fractions (thousandths, millionths, and billionths).

The truth is you don't really need to remember the underlying foundation of these units to make informed decisions, it's only their relative weight that matters. Thus, an 80 GB (gigabyte) hard drive has four times as much storage capacity as a 20 GB hard drive. Both drives store many billions of bytes (1 GB = 1 billion bytes), but you don't need to worry about the value of a billion or the meaning of a byte to compare prices and pick a hard drive off the shelf. Just for the record, a byte can store a numerical value between 0 and 255, which can be interpreted as a letter or symbol according to a standard code.

The average word in this book is a little less than six bytes in length, and the smallest hard drive available can hold thousands of full-length novels. The most important figure of merit for all computer parts is measured in tens or hundreds of dollars. Rather than presenting all the units associated with computer parts and expecting you to memorize them, we'll simply explain the units each time they are encountered and include them in a table at the end of the chapter for reference.

The basic parts in a computer are all dependant on each other to carry out their functions. For example, all the parts depend on the power supply for electrical current at the required voltage levels, and some parts, like the central processing unit and memory, are dependant on the motherboard (main circuit board) to further refine that power for them. This makes it difficult to explain the functions of these parts without referring to others, so we will tackle them in an order that minimizes confusion.

All in all, there are somewhere between 10 and 15 distinct parts involved in a PC build, including the monitor, keyboard, and mouse. By distinct parts, we mean components you pick off a store shelf or order over the phone or Internet. Assembling all these parts to create a working PC will require you to make about 10 push-together connections and screw in 20 or 30 screws, four here, six there, nothing complicated.

Case and Power Supply

The case is almost universally sold with the power supply installed and included in the price. You can build a PC on a workbench without a case (technicians often do this when testing parts), but it takes up a lot of space, interferes with the radio, and is awfully hard to pick up and move in one trip. The function of the case is to house all the parts that make up your PC, provide ventilation for the heat they generate, and protect the local environment from radio frequency interference.

All electrical devices that produce radio frequency emissions are required by law to be certified by the Federal Communications Commission (FCC) as noninterfering with assigned broadcast frequencies. Computers produce a lot of radio frequency "noise" in the FM radio band and higher, but at very low power levels. Normally, if a computer in your home interferes with a radio or television, moving it to another room or even just changing its position by a couple feet will fix the problem.

Computer parts are sold as being FCC Class A or B approved. Class A is for business use, the Class B rating meets more stringent limits for residential use. Assembling a collection of approved parts is no guarantee that the completed computer would pass an FCC test suite for one rating or the other, but as a home hobbyist, you aren't required to have your computer tested. However, if you decide you love building PCs so much that you want to go into business selling thousands of them, you'll want to buy partially assembled or packaged systems that come with an FCC approval sticker.

The power supply, which we lump together with the case because they are sold together, has two basic functions. The primary function is to supply electrical current to all the PC components at the proper, regulated voltage levels. Computer parts require a variety of direct current (DC) voltages, none of which exceed 12 volts, but the power supply itself operates on alternating current (VAC) from the wall socket, so you never want to remove the sealed cover or stick a screwdriver in through the fan grille.

Power supplies are equipped with a 115V/230V switch, so they can be set to 230 volts for Europe and most other regions of the world that don't use the U.S. standard 115 VAC distribution system. Just a few years ago, this 115 or 230 volts was wired directly to the switch on the front of the PC, like the switch on a lamp or a toaster oven. However, in all new PCs, the high voltage never leaves the power supply. The switch on the front panel is really just a logic switch that closes a circuit on the motherboard, which tells the power supply to come on at full power. The power supply is always providing a trickle of current to the motherboard to enable this "wake up" logic, whether the signal is generated by the power switch or by incoming traffic to the modem or network card.

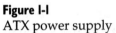

Figure 1-1
ATX power supply

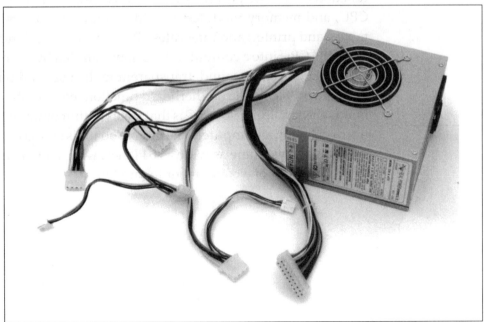

The second function of the power supply is to generate a cooling airflow for both itself and the other parts in the case. This fan in the power supply is the main source of noise coming from most PCs. The manufacturers of the newest high-speed components often recommend that you include additional fans in the case to increase the cooling airflow. The most common location of a single additional fan is at the bottom of the front of the case, to draw in air. A second fan can be added under the power supply at the back of the PC to exhaust more hot air. The goal is always to increase the airflow through the case, not just to blow hot air in a circle, so don't install several fans to draw air into the case and none to exhaust it, or vice versa.

Motherboard

The motherboard, or *mainboard*, is normally the first component to be installed in the case. All additional adapters will be installed directly on the motherboard, and storage devices (drives) will be attached to it by wide ribbon cables. There are a dozen well-known motherboard manufacturers and hundreds of lesser-known brands. PCs are not named for their motherboards, but by their CPUs, such as Pentium 4 or Athlon. The CPU and the memory (RAM) require no connections to anything else in the case other than the motherboard, and can therefore be mounted on the motherboard before it is installed in the case. Not surprisingly, the motherboard is the largest component you will install in the case, and is often the most expensive.

The modern ATX (AT eXtension) motherboard provides many basic functions: It passes power from the power supply to the installed adapters, CPU, and memory modules; provides connection ports for the keyboard, mouse and printer; and integrates all the supporting functions necessary to make the CPU into a computer. Most jobs handled by the motherboard go on entirely in the background, transparent to the user and remarked on only if there is a problem. The motherboard function that you should always keep in mind when building your PC is that it acts as the communications infrastructure for the entire computer. The motherboard is crisscrossed by information superhighways, some as wide as 64 lanes, which move information and instructions from one component to another.

Figure I-2
Motherboard
I/O core

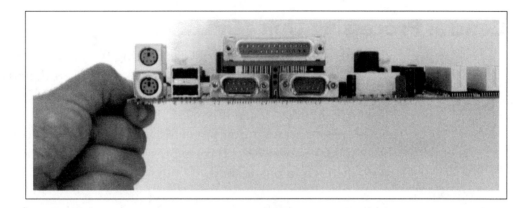

For example, to display a checkbook ledger stored on your system last week, the CPU (which does most of the decision making) asks the hard drive, via a motherboard superhighway, to send this information to immediate memory for use. The requested information is moved from the hard drive to the memory (RAM) via a motherboard superhighway, where the CPU operates on it via a special expressway and formats it for presentation. The information is then sent via another superhighway to the video adapter, which translates it into television-type signals for the monitor. You don't have to keep track of which superhighway, called a *bus*, is involved in every operation, but it is important to understand that the various push-together connections you will make to the motherboard form vital bridges for the information flow.

Motherboards are not designed by manufacturers in a "reinventing the wheel" process. The design of the motherboard is largely controlled by the choice of the chipset—the one or two highly integrated chips that support the CPU. Although the CPU can be seen as the decision maker, it doesn't actually carry out the policing of all the motherboard superhighways (and back roads) by itself. The chipset handles all the support functions for the motherboard, largely in automatic mode, just like nervous system of the human body maintains our vital functions even while we sleep. The level of support offered by the chipset defines the capabilities that can be built into the motherboard, including what speeds will be possible for the CPU and memory. There are far fewer chipset manufacturers than motherboard manufacturers, and CPU manufacturers always design a companion chipset of their own to go with their CPUs.

Central Processing Unit (CPU)

The CPU is the brain of your PC, executing the instructions of the software programs you run, such as Windows XP, Linux, Word, and Quicken. Most PCs are referred to by their CPU and speed, such as a "2 GHz Pentium 4" or a "1.4 GHz Athlon." Currently, all CPUs being manufactured for use in PCs run at speeds from a minimum of 500 megahertz (MHz) to more than 2 gigahertz (GHz), where *hertz* (Hz) expresses the number clock cycles the CPU steps through in one second.

If you should ask, "What can a CPU do in a single step?" the answer is "It depends on the CPU." All CPUs can actually do several things at the same time, and the designers squeeze every drop of performance they can out of a clock cycle. Although it's no longer true that equivalent speed ratings for Intel and AMD CPUs express equivalent performance, the numbers are valid for comparing performance within a family of CPUs. Thus, a 2 GHz Pentium 4 can execute 33 percent more instructions/second than a 1.5 GHz Pentium 4. We'll talk more about how the speed of the CPU impacts the overall performance of the PC in the next chapter.

Figure 1-3
Intel Celeron CPU

One of the biggest bottlenecks to CPU performance is memory speed. These huge numbers for CPU speed we are casually throwing around don't mean much of anything unless the CPU can be supplied with instructions to carry out and data to operate on. To minimize the amount of time CPUs spend waiting for memory, small amounts of super-fast memory called *cache* are included in the CPU package. The Athlon has the biggest cache at 384 KB, followed by the Pentium 4, the Pentium III, the Duron, and the Celeron. Depending on the type of work the CPU is doing, it might find as much as 90 percent of the data it is looking for in cache. Considering that the CPU cache is likely to amount to less than 1 percent of the total system memory, that's a pretty good hit rate.

System Memory or RAM

Random Access Memory (RAM) provides the fast, temporary storage from which your CPU draws the data it needs to operate. The storage capacity of RAM is measured in megabytes (millions of bytes). You'll want to build your new PC with an absolute minimum of 64 MB of RAM. If you are running very demanding applications or high data throughput jobs like video editing, you might want to install as much memory as you can afford. Currently, 256 MB is a pretty healthy amount, and is more than is included in most PCs sold in stores.

There are three basic families of RAM in use today, and we give an example of each with our three builds. The Dynamic RAM (DRAM) that makes up the system memory actually starts to forget everything many times a second, but a dedicated memory controller endlessly reads and writes this information to keep it fresh. Memory, amusingly enough, does forget everything the moment the PC is turned off, which is why we have hard drives, CDs, and floppies to provide storage. The fastest way to tip off a showroom vulture that you are a little hazy about computer terminology is to refer to "the memory in the hard drive."

Floppy Drives

Floppy drives have been around almost as long as the reel-to-reel tape drives that played such a big role in 1960s movies, in which the reels spinning back and forth showed that the computer was "thinking." The 1.44 MB floppy drive that is still standard in the majority of PCs has been around for about 15 years. Floppy drives once played a critical part in getting new PCs up and running, but this role has been replaced by bootable CDs. Exchange of infected floppies remains a possible way to contract a computer virus, but downloading infected files from the Internet is a far more common transmission method.

The 3.5" floppy disk in its hard plastic cartridge is still a convenient way to make a backup copy of your novel or your checkbook register, but because of their relatively low reliability, I keep more than one copy around. The actual recording media is a thin plastic disc with a magnetic coating on each side and a protective coating on top. As with tape drives, the read/write head actually comes in contact with the media. Often, a floppy disk written in one PC will be unreadable in another due to poor manufacturing tolerances, so make sure you try reading your backup floppies in another PC before putting any great confidence in them.

Figure 1-4
Floppy drive

Hard Drives

The most important storage device in your PC is the hard drive. The average hard drive sold today can store as much information as tens of thousands of floppy disks, and it can find and read that information faster than any other storage device, including CDs and DVDs. The majority of the storage space on most people's hard drive is used for programs such as the operating system, word processing and database software, and games. No author, living or dead, could ever fill up a modern hard drive by writing books, but a couple hours of high-quality video would do the job. Although you can always make room on a nearly full hard drive by destroying (deleting) old programs or information, most people prefer to let the clutter build up like old boxes in the attic, simply adding a new hard drive when things get too crowded.

Although the storage provided by the hard drive is certainly permanent in comparison to RAM, it's nowhere near bulletproof. The mean time between failures (MTBF) ratings provided by hard drive manufacturers are highly optimistic, and always exceed the useful life of the drive by at least a decade. Anecdotally, I would estimate that one in ten hard drives suffers complete failure within a couple years of being purchased, with an even higher rate in notebook computers. These failures can result from all sorts of environmental issues such as excessive heat, power spikes, or the PC getting thumped at just the wrong moment.

For this reason, anybody who uses a PC for more than games and Internet surfing should get in the habit of making copies of important information, a process known as "creating a backup." Creating a backup can be as simple as copying your checkbook register or word processing documents to a floppy disk once a week, but never use the floppy disks to exclusively store documents in place of the hard drive because they are far less reliable, not to mention much slower.

Figure 1-5
Inside the
hard drive

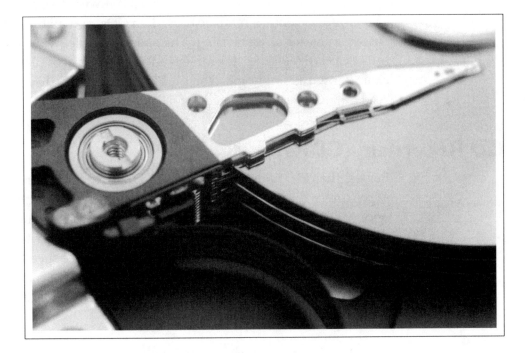

In critical business applications, a special technology called RAID (Redundant Array of Inexpensive Drives) provides a means to duplicate data across several hard drives to increase performance and protect against the failure of any individual drive. RAID solutions usually provide automatic failover, so you won't experience any down time if a single drive fails in the middle of the business day. We will give an example of a simple RAID subsystem in our Pentium 4 build.

RAID provides no protection against fire, theft, data management errors, or computer viruses. Tape backups are the dominant device for backing up large amounts of data, although DVD recorders and new high-capacity cartridge drives from Iomega might pick up some of the load. CD recorders, also know as *burners*, provide an excellent option for data backup if you organize your files on the hard drive so you know what to copy to the CD.

CD Drives

CDs were first developed by the music industry to compete with, then replace, vinyl records. The CD drives in PCs are all capable of playing music CDs without the aid of any other hardware, and most come with a headphone jack right on the front of the drive. A CD holds a three mile-long spiral of information, where the location of a particular item is measured in minutes and seconds from the beginning, as if it were being played in a stereo. The difference between music CDs, data CDs, and all the various hybrids is strictly a matter of formatting. The speed at which your computer plays a music CD is fixed to be the same speed at which stereos play CDs, and this became known as single speed or 1X. The standard CD drives in use today can read data CDs at peak speeds of 50X or faster.

CD Recorders (CDRs)

For less than $100 you can purchase a CDR drive that can record or play CDs. There are two varieties of CD blanks: the older type, which can be written once (CDR) and the newer type, which can be erased and rewritten many times (CDRW). All the production CDR drives can write to either type of blank, which is why the drives are labeled with three speeds: write speed, rewrite speed, and read speed. Blank CDs of either type cost less than 50 cents when you buy them in quantity. The hard plastic CD holders, known as jewel cases, cost as much as the CDs do.

CD recorders are the best way invented yet of transferring large amounts of data between computers that aren't wired together on a fast network. The thing that makes CDs so ideal is that the standard was born outside the PC world, so any type of computer can read a data CD created in any other. The only trick is this: When you are recording music CDs to play in a stereo or data CDs as backups, use the write-only CDR media. The rewritable media (CDRW) is not compatible with all types of readers.

Figure 1-6
An 8X write,
4X rewrite CD
recorder

DVD Drives and Recorders

Digital Video Discs (DVDs) are another entertainment industry innovation, designed primarily to increase the quality of movies viewed at home and reduce the pirating that goes on with VHS tapes. DVDs held about as much information as seven CDs in their first incarnation, and about 28 times as much in their double-sided, double-layered version. DVD drives can read CDs, so there's no reason to put both types of disc readers in a new PC. However, DVD recorders are relatively expensive, costing several times as much as CD recorders, so building a PC with a CDR for recording and a DVD for playing is a common compromise.

The current combination drives (CDR and DVD) are more expensive than buying the drives separately, and the standard DVD drive costs about twice as much as the CD drive. On the other hand, unless you intend to watch movies on your PC, there aren't that many software titles that require DVDs, so you can always build your PC without one and add it later (when the price drops) if the need arises.

Tape Drives

Tape drives are still the number one solution for backing up business computer systems, although they never caught on in home PCs because of the cost and the unfriendly software. One problem with tape drives is that they are far from foolproof. Even professional network administrators sometimes fall into the trap of shuffling tapes each morning and assuming that the backup software is performing its job, only to find there is a problem with restoring the data when a disaster occurs. The danger is greatest when multiple tapes are introduced along with partial backups, in which the tape software only copies files that have changed since the last backup. The only way to make sure your backups are good is to do an occasional restore as a test.

Another problem with tape backups is you need a PC with a working tape drive and the proper tape software to recover files, as opposed to a CD, which can be read anywhere. Unlike all other storage media, which uses some variation of a rotating disk to allow any data to be positioned under the read head almost immediately, tapes need to be wound passed the magnetic read head until the data is reached. Restoring a single small file from a tape usually takes several minutes, most of which the drive spends winding tape. Making a new complete backup of a hard drive can take several hours.

Modems

Modems give your home PC the capability to communicate with other computers over the phone lines or cable and satellite TV infrastructure. For most people, this means connecting to the Internet or a private corporate network. Other uses for modems include turning the PC into an answering machine, a fax machine, a voice mail system, or for playing multiuser games.

Modems, compared with most of the other parts in your PC, are extremely slow. The standard telephone modem is capable of receiving 56 Kb/s (kilobits/second), one of the few times you'll see the puny "kilo" prefix in this book. Cable modems offer a substantial improvement over telephone modems—about a 50 fold increase in download speed under ideal conditions—but your local cable company might not provide the service or it might be too pricey.

There are a variety of advanced technology telephone modem technologies, the most popular of which is DSL (Digital Subscriber Line). These fall a little short of the ideal cable modem performance, but in the real world there isn't a whole lot of difference. Because cable bandwidth is shared within a neighborhood, your performance will drop if many neighbors install (and use) cable modems. DSL is not available everywhere, and even if you know people with DSL who use the same local phone company as you, you might be too far from the central phone office to get it yourself.

Figure 1-7
56 Kb/s modem

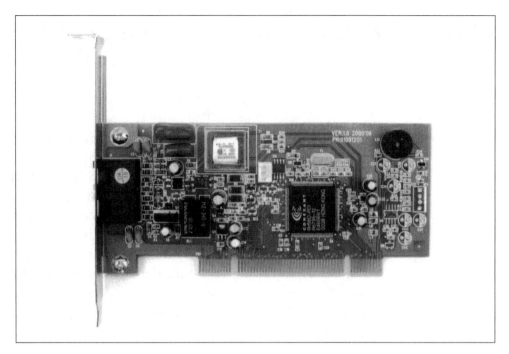

Network Adapter

Everyone who works in an office environment is familiar with computer networks—or at least with computer networks being down. A network adapter in your PC plays essentially the same role as a modem, but it operates much, much faster. The slowest network adapter operating at 10 Mb/s is almost 200 times faster than the standard telephone modem operating at 56 Kb/s. Although many of the performance numbers tossed around for PCs have very little to do with the overall user experience, this one does. A slow network adapter can transfer more information in one minute than a standard telephone modem can in three hours.

Network adapters are very inexpensive and are often included as a standard feature on the motherboard, and all the operating systems support networking without requiring a further investment in software. To set up a small home network, you need to buy a network *hub,* a combination of a switch box and a signal conditioner, in which the individual network cables running to the PCs are joined together. A small hub and a few cables will run you less than $100, allowing you to share files, printers, and high-speed Internet access though the cable TV company may charge you extra. You might want to include a network adapter in your PC, even if you never plan to set up a network, in order to be cable modem ready.

USB, FireWire, and I/O (Input/Output) Ports

In the early days of PCs, there were three options for attaching peripherals to a PC. The first necessitated adding an expensive special adapter to the PC, such as a Small Computer Systems Interface (SCSI) card, which we'll talk about in the next chapter. The other two options were the standard printer port and the two standard serial ports. The printer port has undergone several upgrades to provide higher speeds and enhanced two-way communications, allowing for a variety of peripherals to be attached.

The serial ports have fallen almost completely out of use, especially since the introduction of a separate mouse port. About the only peripherals still using serial ports are some early digital cameras, PDAs, and the rarely used external telephone modem. With the introduction of the home PC, a new type of I/O port was introduced for using a joystick to play computer games. The game port is standard on sound cards or included in the motherboard I/O core if the motherboard has built-in sound.

As the number of high-speed, inexpensive devices available for attachment to the PC multiplied, an equally inexpensive way of attaching them was required. Universal Serial Bus (USB) is a true plug-and-play solution for attaching peripherals. You don't need to turn the PC off to attach or detach USB devices, and the software support in recent operating system releases is seamless.

All new motherboards come standard with two or more USB ports, and large numbers of USB devices can be connected to a single port using a USB hub. The single drawback with the current USB standard (version 1.1) is that at a maximum speed of 12 Mb/s, it's not fast enough to support many high-performance peripherals. That 12 Mb/s (megabits/second) translates into just 1.5 MB/s (megabytes/second), which is nowhere near fast enough to connect even the slowest external hard drives.

There are two competing standards to replace USB 1.1, FireWire and USB 2.0. FireWire (IEEE 1394) has been around for years and has had great success in the multimedia storage markets. At a maximum speed of 400 Mb/s, it has more than enough bandwidth to keep the data moving, and it has the advantage of existing software support. USB 2.0 sports a maximum speed of 480 Mb/, and backward compatibility with existing USB 1.1 devices.

Figure I-8
Adaptec USB 2.0
adapter

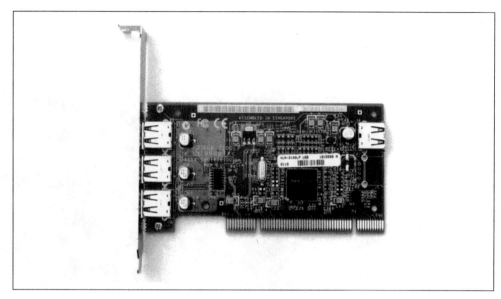

Sound Cards and Speakers

A sound card translates the digital data stored on your PC or downloaded from the Internet into the analog sound waves you can hear, a process called *Digital-to-Analog* (D/A) conversion. Sound cards can also convert analog sound such as music or speech into digital data that can be stored or manipulated by the PC, a process called *Analog-to-Digital* (A/D) conversion. The primary features differentiating sound systems are the power and clarity of their amplifiers and speakers (i.e., Will your PC sound as good as your stereo?).

On a fixed budget, it makes more sense to buy a cheap sound card and expensive speakers. Marketing for sound cards focuses in their 3D effects, wave table sound, and polyphony capabilities. All these are relevant for musicians who will generate or mix music on their PCs, and for game players, but have nothing to do with how a music CD played on a PC will sound. Wave table sound allows the sound card to play a type of compressed music commonly used in games and multimedia presentations, in which the "true" waveform of the desired sound is formed from the wave table. Polyphony refers to how many independent sound streams the card can produce and mix at one instant.

Figure 1-9
PCI sound card

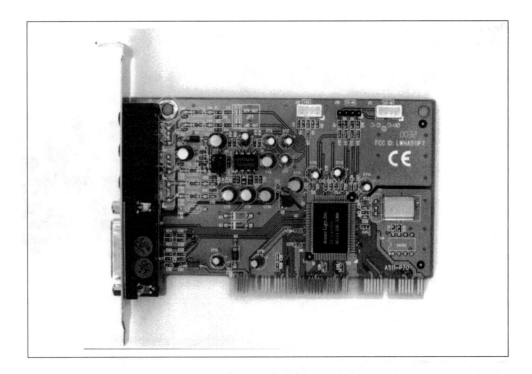

The up-and-coming use for sound cards in PC systems is for speech recognition. That is, talking to your PC. Speech recognition allows for hands-off operation of your computer, with dictation-to-type being the leading application. The technology is rapidly improving and finding acceptance with professionals in challenging environments such as medical and legal practices. Sound card capabilities are the most common candidate for integration on the motherboard, and two of the three PCs in this book required no sound adapter.

Keyboard and Mouse

Two of the cheapest peripherals attached to any computer are the keyboard and mouse, which taken together can cost less than $20. If there is any correlation between the cost of keyboards and their quality, it's been my experience that the cheap keyboards last longer than the expensive ones. Mice, on the other hand, are generally a little nicer as you move up the price ladder, but all mechanical mice require the occasional cleaning. Cleaning the mouse is a five-minute job, usually undertaken when the mouse pointer on the screen insists on only moving up and down when you're trying to go left or right. Turn the mouse upside down, follow the direction arrow to pop off the ball retainer and clean the lint off the two sets of rollers in the mouse. Keyboards are available in a variety of styles, from the 104/105 key rectangular keyboard to the split "V" keyboard and the oversize "surfer" keyboard with dedicated Internet keys.

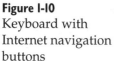

Figure I-I0
Keyboard with
Internet navigation
buttons

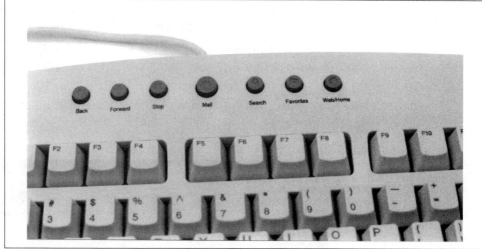

The Video Monitor

A large video monitor can be the most expensive component of a basic PC, which isn't such a bad thing because it's the only piece of hardware other than the printer that comes anywhere near holding its value over time. A monitor is similar to an artist's canvas in that it presents no images or information on its own. It needs to be painted by a remote hand; in this case the video adapter. The video adapter installed in your PC might cost only 20 percent as much as the monitor, yet it controls the resolution and the number of colors displayed.

Monitors, like televisions, are described by the diagonal measurement of the picture tube, in inches. All things being equal, when a 17" monitor displays the same image as a 14" monitor, the picture or text is nearly 50 percent larger. However, the true viewable area of a monitor rarely reaches the actual picture tube measurements, depending on how much of the tube is covered by the plastic housing and whether the monitor controls allow you to adjust the picture out to the edges. A basic understanding of the internal workings of a monitor is nice to have, but if you are buying inexpensive components, you don't need to worry about it. The following paragraph does not apply to the newer LCD or plasma flat screens, which employ all digital technology.

The data to be displayed on the monitor screen is first converted from digital to analog form (from bits to waves) by the video adapter. These waves use varying voltage levels to describe the intensity for red, green, and blue electron guns to fire in order to paint each point on the display, along with a synchronizing signal. The monitor electronics steer the beams from these electron guns by use of magnetic fields (also called *lenses*), which deflect the beams down and across the screen at speeds determined by the horizontal and vertical refresh frequencies. The vertical refresh rate describes how many times the entire screen is redrawn in a second, and the horizontal frequency must be fast enough to steer the beam all the way across the screen enough times to paint every *pixel* (point on the screen) in a single vertical scan. These refresh frequencies are included in the product information sheet for every monitor, and the higher numbers usually mean better quality.

Figure 1-11
17" monitor displaying two pages of text

Pixels provide a measure of image resolution (detail), with no dependence on the monitor used. A picture made up from a grid of 640 horizontal points and 480 vertical points (640×480) is the lowest quality image (plain VGA) used on computers today, and even this is appreciably sharper than a standard TV picture. Even the least expensive monitors used today can display much higher resolution (finer) images than this, but for many people, an inexpensive monitor flickers noticeably when pushed to the higher resolutions. The main factor controlling monitor flicker is the vertical refresh rate; a monitor capable of 75–85 redraws per second (75Hz or higher) at a given resolution will produce a really solid picture.

The sharpness of the images painted is dependent on the *dot pitch* or *stripe pitch* of the monitor phosphor. The *pitch* is a measure, in millimeters, of the distance between two phosphor dots or stripes of the same color on the inside surface of the monitor screen. Some manufacturers use an aperture or mask pitch measurement that actually describes the size of the holes in part of the beam focusing train, but an equivalent dot pitch measurement should be available. Likewise, LCD screens give an equivalent dot pitch number, although no electron beams or phosphor are involved. The smaller the dot pitch, the finer the image, although there might be a trade-off in brightness.

Video Adapters

When it comes to choosing a video adapter, the Advanced Graphics Port (AGP) design is the only way to go. The main figure of merit for these adapters is the amount of video RAM they sport and the speed of the special purpose video signal processor. AGP adapters also have a basic speed rating of 1X, 2X, or 4X, which describes the maximum data transfer rate they can achieve in ideal circumstances, although the slower 1X and 2X adapters are disappearing from the market.

You can spend a lot of money on a video adapter for rapidly rendering high-resolution 3D images for animation. These adapters find their primary applications in heavy imaging environments in which the product is the picture, such as medical imaging; multimedia production; and of course, games. For most home users, the standard $30 AGP adapter is more than adequate, and in some cases less prone to compatibility problems than adapters costing 20 times as much. A popular feature on many video cards is a television tuner, which effectively turns your PC into a TV.

Figure 1-12
4X AGP video adapter with 32 MB RAM

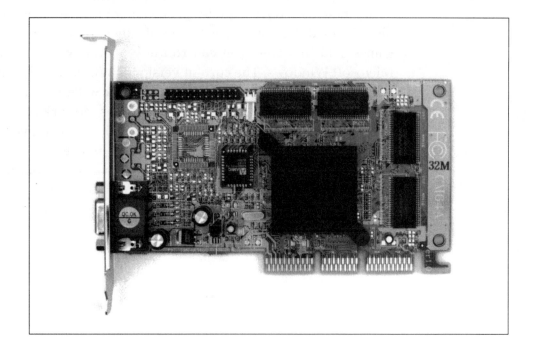

Many new motherboards come with *onboard* video, an AGP adapter and connection port integrated into the motherboard, which eliminates the need for an add-in adapter. Surprisingly, these motherboards often cost less than similar motherboards without video capabilities. We used a motherboard such as this for the Pentium III/Celeron build in this book, but we should point out that there are three drawbacks:

❏ The capabilities of the integrated video controller are often limited in comparison to even the most inexpensive video adapters.

❏ The video adapter shares the main memory on the motherboard with the system. This means if you have limited amount of memory installed, you are giving some of it up to the video controller.

❏ Manufacturers of motherboards with an integrated AGP controller don't include an AGP slot for an add-in adapter. Therefore, if the onboard video controller is too slow or fails, you can't replace it with a standard AGP adapter; you'll have to fall back on an older PCI (Peripheral Component Interface) model.

Operating Systems

For most PC builders, the choice of operating system is similar to Henry Ford's famous Model T quote, "You can get it in any color, as long as it's black." For those who want to run all the shrink-wrapped software and games sold in stores, you can run any operating system as long as it's Microsoft Windows. The current version is Windows XP, available in both home and business versions, but some people will prefer to install the older versions with which they are familiar, such as Me, 2000, NT, 98, or even 95. The standard bearer of the "Anybody but Microsoft" movement continues to be the freeware Linux operating system, but its market penetration is largely limited to servers and techies. There are hundreds of excellent freeware applications that run under Linux, but don't expect to see it listed on the side of the Microsoft Office box any time soon.

Unit Shorthand	Unit Written Out	Actual Value	Applies To	Nominal Range
b	Bit	0 or 1, expressed as a voltage level	Bus width, memory module width	8, 16, 32, 64, 128, 256
B	Byte	8 bits, an unsigned number between 0 and 255	Basic unit of capacity	Byte, kilobyte, megabyte, gigabyte
KB	Kilobyte	1,000 bytes (rounded from 1,024)	File size	1 KB to many MBs
MB	Megabyte	1 million bytes	Capacity for memory modules, CDs, floppies	1 MB–1 GB
GB	Gigabyte	1 billion bytes	Capacity, hard drives, DVDs	1Gb to terabytes
Kb/s	Kilobits/second	1000 bits per second	Modem and I/O port speeds	9,600–112 Kb/s
Mb/s	Megabits/second	1million bits per second	Network and serial bus transfer speeds	10–480 Mb/s
KB/s	Kilobytes/second	1000 bytes per second	File download speed via modem	1–10 KB/s
MB/s	Megabytes/second	1 million bytes per second	Bus (SCSI, IDE, PCI, AGP) transfer speed	3–1,066 MB/s
MHz	Megahertz	1 million cycles per second	CPU clock, bus clock	33–1,000 MHz
GHz	Gigahertz	1 billion cycles per second	CPU clock	1–3 GHz
ms	Milliseconds	1/1000 of a second	Drive seek time, keyboard repeat rate	5–300 ms
ns	Nanosecond	1 billionth of a second	Memory access time	6–70 ns
d	Dot	A unique point	Computer screens	0.25–0.31mm (as in dot pitch of screen)
dpi	Dots per inch	Dots printed or scanned from a linear inch	Printers, scanner	100–2,400 dpi
$	Dollars	100 cents	All PC components	$5 for a mouse to hundreds for high-end parts

Chapter 2

Selecting and Purchasing Parts

In this chapter we review the basic component choices you need to make before you begin purchasing parts. If you already have some experience with assembling PCs, the relationships between these parts will already be clear to you. If not, we suggest you take some time now to browse through the assembly photographs in Chapters 4–7 to see how PCs are actually put together. This will give you a little familiarity with the physical appearance of the parts, along with the sizing relationships and connections that will be made between the components. We actually introduce the subject of shopping for parts before selecting them, because finding good pricing has a lot to do with which parts you can afford to select.

There are two major sources for buying computer parts at good prices, and each has its advantages and disadvantages. The first source is mail order based on print advertisements or Internet sites. The main advantages of mail order are price, unlimited selection, and the security inherent in credit card transactions. The hidden time bomb of mail-order purchasing is shipping costs and turnaround time, both the initial cost to get the parts to you and any reshipping costs and delays due to mistakes or defective merchandise.

One way to minimize shipping costs is to buy all your parts from the same mail-order supplier. However, you must clearly state at the time of your order that you will not accept partial shipment, or the delivery charges could start mounting up. Even worse, your order might show up lacking some critical component that could be another week in coming, effectively postponing the build. In extreme cases, partial shipments may be accepted and paid for, only for the supplier to call two weeks later and inform you they no longer stock the missing part at all. Another problem with some mail-order outlets is that the prices you are quoted may mysteriously creep up a few bucks here and there. This will generally be attributed to "a problem in the system," but by reading your invoice and complaining to your credit card company, you can be sure to pay what you intended.

The other source for reasonably priced computer parts is retail computer stores and superstore chains. The superstores have the advantage of volume buying power, particularly on boxed items that move quickly such as printers, monitors, scanners, and CD recorders. Manufacturer and store rebates are another way to lower your component cost at superstores, and on the whole, rebate fulfillment has improved over the last five years or so. Still, it pays to make a photocopy of the rebate paperwork in case it falls between the cracks.

The friendly neighborhood computer shop is a much better source for advice and will probably carry a greater variety of CPUs, motherboards, and cases. The neighborhood shop will also be able to order any special parts for you, although not as cheaply as you could get them through direct mail order. The main advantage of retail stores is that if you get defective part, you can pop back in and return it for another one, usually hassle free. You can't expect to get a good deal on all your parts in a retail store. They are particularly bad on items such as memory, video adapters, and cables, but they often sell hard drives and CDRs as loss leaders to get you in the door.

Computer shows were once a major source of parts, combining mail-order pricing with retail availability. In fact, the pricing of vendors at some shows was so aggressive that you had to wonder if their merchandise fell off a truck. Aside from pricing, the main advantage of shows was you could really get your hands on the parts you were buying. Often the vendor would have an open PC at the table to stick the parts in and prove they were working. They also handed out plenty of free advice about what you wanted and why, and you could see a lot of things you would buy if money were no object.

However, the popularity of these shows has died down with the maturity of the industry, and there were several problems associated with them. One drawback was that the cost for a fly-by-night outfit to set up a booth at a computer show for the weekend was appreciably less than the cost of an ad in a magazine. This meant that anybody with $100 in his pocket could set up a "Moe's Computer" sign, sell you stuff with a three-year warranty, and then disappear off the face of the earth on Monday morning. Another drawback was the frenetic show atmosphere that can lead to hasty purchasing decisions and leave shoppers vulnerable to high-pressure sales tactics.

Monitors, printers, and other peripherals should be purchased locally whenever possible. The shipping costs for these often exceed $30, depending on your location, and you should be able to get a decent deal at the local office superstore or computer chain store. There are search engines on the Internet specifically geared toward helping you shop for parts. The most popular is probably Pricewatch (www.pricewatch.com), but you can also try www.streetprices.com or www.zdnet.com/computershopper. *Computer Shopper* magazine from Ziff-Davis remains a good source for parts, although over the last few years it has slimmed down to a shadow of its former self.

A system including a case, power supply, motherboard, memory, CPU, and video card is generally referred to as a "bare bones system." Even without any drives or other adapters installed, you can attach a monitor to a bare bones system and get a live screen. There are big advantages to buying the bare bones of your system from a single source. First of all, that supplier accepts responsibility that the components you have chosen will work together when assembled properly. This means you won't end up with a CPU not supported by your motherboard or the wrong voltage AGP video adapter. Another advantage is that if you have difficulty getting your assembled system to work, your vendor can't try to shift the blame to other suppliers.

Paying for Performance

To do full justice to all the new technologies and variations that are used in today's PCs, we would have to triple or quadruple the number of pages in this book, and then you would have to sift through them! Our compromise is to supply enough information to enable you to make educated buying decisions for parts without trying to invade the turf of PC magazines, whose primary mission is to provide reviews of the latest and greatest hardware. There are also some excellent Web sites that post daily reviews of PC components, most notably Tom's Hardware Guide (www.tomshardware.com) and Anand Tech (www.anandtech.com).

You don't need to master all the terms and technology in this chapter to build a PC. In fact, the actual assembly job requires very little knowledge about the technology and performance of the individual parts. Good vendors can help you choose the right combination of components to meet your performance needs and budget, but beware they will interpret "meeting the budget" as "spending all the money allotted." No book can make you a purchasing expert until you get some hands-on experience, but hopefully the information in this chapter will help you ask the right questions before you lay out your hard-earned cash.

The toughest question you must ask yourself when purchasing parts for your PC is, "How much performance do I need today?" There is no point in trying to cover any possible future needs with what you buy today, particularly since you are building your own PC and can easily upgrade it a year from now when that $400 CPU you were looking at costs less than $100. Many of the standard-size computer parts sold today far exceed the average demand. For example, the vast majority of PCs currently in use have hard drives smaller than 10 GB, and most people never fill these up. Yet, the average hard drive sold today has a capacity of 30 GB or more and costs less than 3 GB drives cost when they were popular a couple years ago. If you plan to record a lot of music or store thousands of high-resolution images, by all means, buy the largest hard drive on the market. If not, buy the 30 GB drive with the rebate.

The dirty little secret of the PC industry is that performance increases are rarely cumulative. In other words, if you select five components (a CPU, a hard drive, a CD-ROM, a video adapter, and RAM), each of which guarantees you a 20 percent increase in performance over the lower priced versions of the same, you won't end up with a PC that's 100 percent faster. You're more likely to end up with a PC that's 20 percent faster, some of the time. Why not all the time? Well, if you spend a lot of time surfing the Web, the pages aren't going to load any faster. The limiting factor there is the 56 Kb/s modem, and a slow computer with a cable modem will blow the doors off a fast computer with telephone modem when it comes to Web surfing. If you print a lot of color pictures on your inkjet, they won't print any faster. The real bottleneck here is the printer itself. What is cumulative about the five "high-performance" parts is the price. That hypothetical PC will cost twice as much. In fact, unless you are an avid game player pushing motion 3D graphics to their limit, your PC spends most of its time waiting for you to ask it to do something.

Selecting a CPU

In the first chapter we introduced cases, power supplies, and motherboards before CPUs, because without these, the CPU is helpless. However, when it comes to purchasing the parts to build a system, the choice of CPU controls which motherboard, power supply, and memory you will require. There are two real players in the CPU manufacturing game: Intel and Advanced Micro

Devices (AMD). Intel retains the lion's share of the market, especially in the business world where brand recognition is king, but AMD is steadily gaining in popularity with home PC builders and gamers.

Intel's flagship processor in the PC market is the Pentium 4. The Pentium 4 is available for two different families of motherboards: Socket 423 and Socket 478. Intel's Pentium III is still a popular CPU, as is the low-cost Celeron, and both of these are available for Socket 370 motherboards, although you might still encounter some Slot 1 motherboard units.

The AMD Athlon XP compares well with the fastest Pentium 4s in most applications, despite the Pentium 4's higher clock speeds. The Duron, AMD's low-cost processor, is more than powerful enough for the majority of users. Both of the AMD CPUs are designed for Socket A motherboards, as the earlier Slot A versions have been phased out. All modern CPUs require an active *heatsink*, a metal finned structure for radiating heat topped by a cooling fan.

Figure 2-1
A CPU active heatsink

CPU prices are structured to take advantage of business buyers for whom a few hundred dollars in cost difference is a small factor in the overall purchasing decision. Never buy the fastest speed CPU within a family of processors, or you'll be paying a couple hundred dollars extra for a speed difference that is impossible to detect in most applications. If you have the extra money to spend, consider using it on options with far more impact, like a large monitor, better printer or video adapter, more memory, or a cable modem.

One of the best reasons for building your own PC is that you can maximize your value without getting stuck paying for the fastest CPU and other parts you don't need. CPUs should not be chosen for their internal architectural design features, which are entirely transparent to the user. Terms like "super scalar," "super pipelined," "multiple branch prediction," and "out-of-order processing" apply to all the current CPU designs and do not offer a rational basis for comparison. All the CPUs discussed in this book are fully x86-compatible (they will work with software written for any PC since the IBM AT) and support the industry standard MMX (MultiMedia eXtension) instructions. This means they will be capable of running any shrink-wrapped PC software you buy.

There really are only three factors to take into consideration when choosing a CPU: the price, speed (in MHz or GHz), and bus support. When comparing CPU pricing, don't forget to take the cost of the motherboard into account. Motherboards for Intel CPUs are produced in higher quantities than those for AMD CPUs. Therefore, their prices are generally lower and can offset some of the cost difference in the CPUs. The speed of a CPU in MHz or GHz is really only relevant when comparing it to an identical CPU at a different speed. Although higher numbers always mean faster, the overall performance gain of the PC as measured by the user's experience comes nowhere near reflecting the increased clock speed.

The other critical choice is the memory bus, or *Front Side Bus* (FSB), support. For example, the best value in high-performance memory is *Double Data Rate* (DDR) technology, which is currently only supported by the AMD CPUs, although the Pentium 4 is due to add this capability by press time.

Intel Pentium 4

The first build in our book is an Intel Pentium 4 at a speed of 2 GHz on a new Socket 478 motherboard, also from Intel. The Pentium 4 is the highest price CPU in this book, and the only build we do with RAMBUS technology memory (more on memory later). The Pentium 4 has a 400 MHz FSB when used with RAMBUS memory, but the bus width is narrower, so the numbers can't be directly compared with other memory bus speeds. The original Pentium 4 was designed for Socket 423, which is appreciably larger than the new Socket 478. You cannot mount a Socket 423 Pentium 4 on a Socket 478 motherboard or vice versa. This shrinking of the socket and the CPU package is made possible by continual advancements in the semiconductor technology, primarily reductions in the actual size of the microscopic transistors on the chip. Intel has developed a new heatsink for the Pentium 4 that is a genuine advancement over the older heatsinks, primarily for its ease of installation.

Figure 2-2
2 GHz Intel
Pentium 4 and
Socket 478

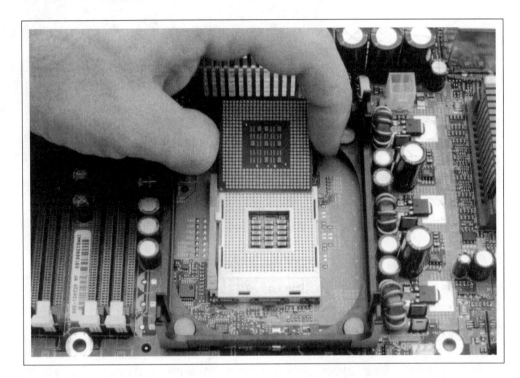

AMD Athlon and Duron

The second build in our book can be configured as either an AMD Athlon or Duron simply by changing the CPU. The Athlon and the Duron for Socket A (also known as Socket 462) are identical in appearance and utilize the same heatsink. The real difference between the Athlon and the Duron, aside from the clock speeds available, is the amount of cache memory on the processor: 384 KB for the Athlon; 192 KB for the Duron. Currently, the Athlon supports the 266 MHz FSB and the Duron only supports the 200 MHz FSB, but this difference is less important than the cache and the clock speed. Beginning with the recently introduced Athlon XP, AMD has established a new performance rating for CPUs, based on benchmark performance rather than the clock speed in megahertz. These new performance ratings offer an equivalent megahertz rating followed by a "+". Depending on the heatsink you purchase, you may need to add a drop of thermal grease to the CPU die. Be careful not drown the CPU; a small drop of thermal grease is sufficient.

Figure 2-3
AMD CPU with
a dab of thermal
grease on the die

Intel Pentium III and Celeron

The third build in our book follows two paths: a Slot 1 Pentium III and a Socket 370 Celeron. This is made possible by the highly integrated motherboard we chose, which sports both types of CPU sockets. The path of Intel processors has been back away from slot-to-socket style CPUs, but Slot 1 motherboards and CPUs are still being sold. The Pentium III CPU, depending on the model, supports either a 100 MHz or a 133 MHz FSB and features 256 KB cache. The early Celeron CPUs, those running at clock speeds up to 533 MHz, are based on the Pentium II core, whereas the faster models are based on the Pentium III. These newer Celerons have been dubbed "Celeron 2" by many parts vendors, but it's not an official Intel designation and they only carry 128 KB cache. All Celeron CPUs are limited to a 66 MHz FSB, which puts them at quite a disadvantage when it comes to moving large amounts of data through memory.

AMD K6 Series CPUs

One of the biggest surprises as I prepared to write this third edition of *Build Your Own PC* is that the AMD K6-2 and K6-3 series CPUs are still being sold. Although these were great CPUs in their day and are still capable of running demanding applications, I'm not quite sure why the faster Duron CPUs at similar price points haven't driven them out of the market. Perhaps it's a question of motherboard cost. The K6 series CPUs require Super 7 motherboards, which likewise are still available through many outlets. If you really want to build one of these, pick up a copy of the first edition of this book (ISBN 0-07-134628-7), in which a K6 series CPU was one of the two featured systems.

Multiprocessor and Workstation CPUs

Given an infinite amount of money, there are two ways to get more performance out of a computer based on the standard PC architecture. One approach is to put multiple CPUs on a special motherboard and run software designed to take advantage of them. Pentium 4 and Pentium III processors have always been supported in multiprocessor configurations, and the Athlon MP is supported by dual-processor Socket A motherboards. Intel has further differentiated the market between PCs and servers with their line of Xeon processors, enhanced versions of the Pentium series CPUs that were priced out of the home PC market. Finally, Intel recently released its Itanium processor, which is aimed squarely at the high-end server and workstation market.

CPU	Package Types Currently Available	Clock Speeds Currently Available[1]	FSB Speed	Basic Price/Top Performance Price
Pentium 4	Socket 478 Socket 423	>1.7 GHz >1.4 GHz	400 MHz with RIMM, 266 MHz (1st Q 2002) with DDR	$200/$500 $100/$300
Athlon XP Athlon	Socket A Socket A	>1.5 GHz + >1 GHz	266 MHz with DDR	$120/$220 $50/$110
Pentium III	Slot 1/Socket 370	>800 MHz	133MHz or 100 MHz	$100/$165
AMD Duron	Socket A	>750 MHz	200 MHz with DDR	$25/$65
Celeron	Socket 370	>550 MHz	66 MHz	$35/$70
AMD K6 series	Socket 7	>500 MHz	66/100 MHz	$20/$45

[1]*The CPUs are available at the speed following the ">" and higher. Earlier generations of the same CPU may have been available at lower speeds. The "+" following the Athlon XP rating indicates an equivalent performance measure, not the actual clock speed.*

Motherboards

The CPU and the motherboard are so interdependent that it's a little unfair to have to put one before the other. As we mentioned earlier, you really shouldn't pick a CPU without considering the motherboard price and available motherboard features in the overall picture. For starters, motherboards that support the older CPUs tend to be loaded with more extras, such as integrated modems and video, than newer motherboards. One reason is that manufacturers in a mature market need to add features to compete. Another reason is that older CPUs are destined for lower-end systems in which cost takes precedence over performance. In fact, mail-order outfits that specialize in motherboard sales always offer a wide variety of motherboards, each with a list of price points for the different speeds of CPUs the board supports. In other words, they consider a CPU to be a motherboard option, and there is a lot of logic in their approach.

The main differentiation between motherboards is their CPU support. Although this information is given in the preceding table, we'll run through it quickly one more time. Socket 478 motherboards and Socket 423 motherboards support Pentium 4 CPUs, depending on which CPU package you use. Socket A motherboards support Athlons and Durons. Socket 370 motherboards support Pentium III and Celeron CPUs and Slot 1 motherboards support the older style cartridge style Pentium IIIs (and older Celerons and Pentium IIs). So, given a variety of motherboards that support the particular CPU you have chosen, the job is to look at the other motherboard features (including price) and pick one.

If you are installing one of the newer, high-performance CPUs, either the Pentium 4 or Athlon, the next most important feature on your shopping list should be memory support. If you're going to make the investment in a Pentium 4, you want a motherboard that supports dual-channel RDRAM or, as should be available soon, Double Data Rate (DDR) memory modules at 266 MHz. If you are shopping for an Athlon motherboard, support for the 266 MHz DDR memory modules is the only way to go. Motherboards for both of these CPUs are available that only support PC133 memory, but that strikes me as being penny wise and pound foolish.

Figure 2-4
Selecting 266 MHz DDR support on an Athlon/Duron motherboard

If you are buying a motherboard for a Pentium III or Celeron, all the motherboards available will probably support PC133 memory, even though the Celeron is limited to operation at 66 MHz. Most new Duron motherboards will support the 266 MHz DDR modules even though the Duron is only capable of running the bus at 200 MHz, but the manufacturers want to be able to fully support the Athlon with the same product.

In all cases, the number of memory modules that can be installed and the total amount of memory supported will vary from motherboard to motherboard, but with memory prices as cheap as they are, the capability to upgrade memory by adding more later has become relatively unimportant. Also, it was never a good idea to mix different brands and speeds of memory modules on a motherboard, and it's actually prohibited with the new RIMMs.

The next big question is "what features you want on the motherboard?" If you already have an AGP video adapter and a sound card in mind, you don't want a motherboard that has these features integrated, even if it's cheaper. For one thing, motherboards with integrated video don't usually have an AGP slot for installing an adapter. Furthermore, disabling onboard functions such as sound doesn't always work out as smoothly as it should.

An integrated network adapter is a great feature, but I wouldn't put too much faith in motherboard modems. You're usually better off with an add-in fax/modem adapter. Pretty much all motherboards come stock with two serial I/O ports and one parallel (printer port), abbreviated 2S/1P; and two USB ports; not to mention PS/2-style keyboard and mouse ports. These ports are all mounted on the back edge of the motherboard, known as the *I/O core*. Today's computer cases normally ship with a universal I/O shield on the back of the case that has punch-out blanks to fit the motherboard's I/O core features. Motherboards with nonstandard I/O cores will ship with a custom I/O shield that can be snapped into place.

If you aren't buying a motherboard with a large number of integrated features, you'll want a number of expansion slots for add-in adapters. Highly integrated motherboards are often extremely stingy with bus slots. The motherboard used in our Pentium III/Celeron build only has two slots, an old ISA slot and a PCI slot, only one of which can be used at a time. There is no standard number and arrangement of slots, although a single 4X AGP slot (we'll talk more about this when we get to video adapters) and a number of PCI slots are the norm. All new add-in adapters (excluding the video card) are PCI adapters.

In some rare cases you might have an old ISA card you need to reuse, but this will greatly narrow your choice of motherboards, because very few support even a single ISA slot. There are two good reasons for choosing a motherboard with twice as many PCI slots as you have adapters to install. First, you will have the flexibility to add adapters later that you might not need at build time. Second, it allows you to put some spacing between your adapters for better air circulation and less cable crowding. The current PCI standard is release 2.2 and supports newer 3.3 V and older 5.0 V adapters.

Figure 2-5
PCI slots

The final two features that differentiate between motherboards and which have more impact on the cost than any of the aforementioned options are embedded SCSI (Small Computer Systems Interface) controllers and multiprocessor support. All new motherboards come equipped with a primary and secondary IDE (Intelligent Drive Electronics) controller capable of 100 MB/s (or DMA/100) transfers, and some even integrate a simple IDE RAID (Redundant Array of Inexpensive Drives) controller. A high-end add-in SCSI adapter can cost $250 or more, so don't be surprised if it adds as much to the cost of a motherboard to have one integrated.

Multiprocessor support can also add a couple hundred dollars to the price of a motherboard, but both SCSI and multiprocessor support are really intended for servers and graphics workstations. We'll talk more about SCSI and RAID later in the chapter, and we illustrate both disk subsystems in our Pentium 4 build.

Brand	CPU support	Features	Price
Intel G850MD Micro ATX	Pentium 4 in Socket 478	4 RIMM, sound, network, 7 USB ports, ATA100	$145
DFI WT70	Pentium 4 in Socket 423	4 RIMM, 6 PCI slots, 2 USB, ATA100, 4X AGP	$135
Soyo SYK7ADA	Athlon/Duron in Socket A	3 DDR slots to 266 MHz, built-in IDE RAID ATA100, 4X AGP	$100
ECS P655AT	Pentium III/Celeron in Socket 370	133MHz bus, ATA100, 5PCI, 4X AGP	$70
Amptron M599LMR	AMD K6-2/III in Super 7	100 MHz bus, 2 PCI/1ISA, onboard AGP, sound, 56 KB/s modem, 10/100BaseT, ATA66	$70

Memory

We try to avoid giving history lectures in this book, but on the subject of memory, a brief review is essential to understanding the terminology. One of the basic innovations that made digital computers possible, *Random Access Memory* (RAM) allows the CPU to retrieve information stored at a specific memory address without having to read through all the memory to find it. Contrast this with a tape drive, where the whole tape may have to be wound by the read head to reach the location of the desired information. Even with the relatively fast hard drive, the read head must physically move, as much as tens of millimeters, and wait for the disk to spin until the information is under the head.

The access times of drives are measure in *milliseconds,* or thousandths of a second; the access time of RAM is measured in *nanoseconds,* or billionths of a second. When it comes to locating a single byte of data at a random location, memory outperforms other storage media by a factor of hundreds of thousands. If this wasn't the case, the super-fast CPUs would have no purpose, because they would spend all their time waiting for new instructions and data to work on.

There are two basic types of RAM in use: *Static RAM* (SRAM) and *Dynamic RAM* (DRAM). Both types of memory forget everything if the power is turned off, but SRAM doesn't require the constant refreshing the DRAM does, ergo the names, "Static" and "Dynamic." SRAM requires four or five times as many transistors to implement as DRAM, as it actually traps each bit of information in a structure called a *flip-flop.* DRAM stores a bit as a temporary charge on the leg of a single transistor, but this decays away so rapidly that it must be reread and refreshed many times per second. SRAM is used as cache memory on CPUs and in other applications, but always in relatively small amounts because of its increased power and real estate demands. DRAM is used for the main PC memory and has been since the original IBM PC was introduced 20 years ago.

Fast Page Memory (FPM) was the first big performance enhancement to DRAM, which had previously treated each new memory transaction like a surprise invitation. FPM made it faster to access data in the same memory "page" although the term "row" offers a better representation of what really goes on. When a new data bit is to come from the same matrix row as the previous bit, the memory controller needs only to increment the column location and the same row address will be used, saving an address transaction.

Extended Data Out (EDO) DRAM shortens the recovery time between sequential DRAM reads, offering about a 20 percent performance boost in overall memory throughput. EDO was backward compatible, meaning it would function in systems that were designed to support FPM RAM, albeit without any performance increase. *Burst EDO* (BEDO) was the next level of enhancement in which a series, or burst, of bytes from memory could be transferred to the CPU in a single request. If the CPU actually required data from these subsequent locations, an operation has been saved, and if not, nothing has been lost.

Synchronous DRAM (SDRAM) can really boost memory bandwidth through synchronization with the system clock. This eliminates a large number of timing delays, which can result in wait states on the part of the CPU (i.e., idle time). The motherboard must be designed to support SDRAM, which is not backward compatible to EDO or FPM. Early SDRAM modules were 5V devices, but the current modules require 3.3V. Fortunately, memory module designers got together early on and came up with a standard system of notches in the contact edge of memory modules, which prevents them from being installed in the wrong type of memory socket. SDRAM was originally available at 66 MHz, but 100 MHz (PC100) and 133 MHz (PC133) devices soon followed. The current speed champion for SDRAM is PC150 (150 MHz) and is popular with overclockers.

Double Data Rate (DDR) SDRAM, simply known as DDR, is the next step after SDRAM. DDR can effectively double the throughput of earlier SDRAMs by transferring data on both the rising and falling edges of the bus clock. The Athlon was the first CPU to take advantage of DDR, which it currently supports with a 266 MHz FSB, and the Pentium 4 is expected to follow suit. The Duron supports DDR at 200 MHz. DDR modules are known both by their MHz rating and PC nomenclature similar to the earlier SDRAM modules. 200 MHz DDR is PC1600, 266 MHz DDR is PC2100, and 300 MHz DDR is PC2400. The motherboard must explicitly support DDR for it to be used.

Figure 2-6
256 MB DDR
DIMM

The RAM used in the IBM PC came in the form of one bit-wide chips in *Dual Inline Packages,* or *DIP Chips.* As memory chips shrank and capacity grew, they were mounted on small circuit boards called *Single Inline Memory Modules* (SIMMs), first 8 bits wide (1 byte) and then 32 bits wide (4 bytes). As chips continued to shrink and capacity and memory buses continued to grow, the SIMM width was doubled, giving us DIMM. The current DIMM modules are 64 bits wide, the same as the memory bus in PC systems not using RDRAM, so they can be installed singly or in any multiple.

RAMBUS, or *RDRAM,* technology represents a departure from the step-by-step evolution of RAM we have presented to this point. *RDRAM Inline Memory Modules* (RIMMs) are only 16 bits wide, but they make up in speed what they lack in width. Dual-channel motherboards operate RIMMs in pairs, allowing an effective width of 32 bits at speeds of up to 800 MHz. Not surprisingly, RDRAM modules run awfully hot, and they currently cost about twice as much as DDR modules of the same capacity.

RIMMs must be installed in banks of two, and unused banks must be filled with special dummies called *Continuity RIMMs* (CRIMMS) for electrical signal continuity. The 800 MHz RIMM is designated PC800; there are also slower versions designated PC700 and PC600, although they are primarily used in mass-market systems.

Figure 2-7
128 MB PC800
RIMM above
CRIMM

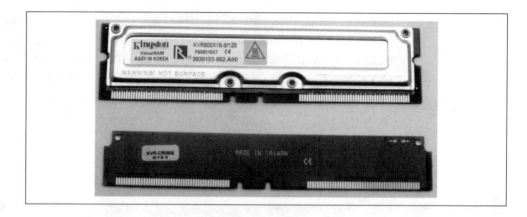

Memory Technology	Designation	Memory Bus Speed	Bus Width	Perfect World Throughput[1]
Dual Channel[2] RDRAM (RIMM)	PC800	400 MHz[3]	32 bits = 4 bytes (requires 2 RIMMs)	3.2 GB/s
	PC700	356 MHz		2.8 GB/s
	PC600	300 MHz		2.4 GB/s
Double Data Rate (DDR)	PC2400	150 MHz[3]	64 bits = 8 bytes	2.4 GB/s
	PC2100	133 MHz		2.1 GB/s
	PC1600	100 MHz		1.6 GB/s
Synchronous Dynamic RAM (SDRAM)	PC150	150 MHz	64 bits = 8 bytes	1.2 GB/s
	PC133	133 MHz		GB/s
	PC100	100 MHz		800 MB/s
	SDRAM	66MHz		528 MB/s

[1] *Perfect world throughput is rarely sustained in practice.*
[2] *Same designations but half the throughput for Single Channel RDRAM (motherboards that allow operation with a single RIMM installed).*
[3] *Data transferred on rising and falling clock, doubling throughput.*

Both DDR and RIMM modules are available with the *Error Correction Code* (ECC) enhancement. ECC memory can correct single-bit errors on the fly and catch multiple-bit errors, unlike the earlier parity error checking, which couldn't correct any errors or identify two-bit flips. ECC memory must be supported by the motherboard, unless it uses ECC onboard technology; and the price premium for ECC memory has almost disappeared with plummeting memory prices.

Video Adapter

There is no good reason to build a new PC with anything less than a 4X *Advanced Graphics Port* (AGP) adapter. The original AGP adapters at 1X (single speed) and 2X were 3.3 Volt devices. The new 2X and 4X AGP adapters (with a single exception I've heard of) are 1.5 Volt devices. Many of the new AGP adapters support either voltage, but motherboards are designed to work at one voltage or the other. Generally speaking, any motherboard that supports 4X AGP will work with a 1.5 Volt AGP adapter.

As with memory modules, AGP adapters are keyed with a notch in their contact edge so they cannot be installed in an AGP slot that doesn't supply the correct voltage. The early 1X/2X AGP adapters have a notch in the connector edge toward the back of the card (the end with the video connector) and the newer 2X/4X cards have a notch toward the front of the connector edge (the front of the case). Universal adapters that support 1.5 or 3.3 Volts at any speed have both notches.

AGP 8X has already been specified, but neither the adapters nor the motherboards to support them existed at press time. Just to make things a little more interesting, there is another variation, AGP Pro, which requires an extension to the video slot toward the back of the case; and a similar addition to the AGP edge connector, called the Pro registration tab. AGP Pro does nothing to widen the AGP bus or increase the bus speed. What it does offer is an increased power supply to power-hungry graphics processors and video RAM, increasing the supply from a baseline of 25 watts to as much as 100 watts. If you go the AGP Pro route, the minimum power supply rating you'll want to consider is 350 watts. The basic clock speed for all AGP slots is 66 MHz, the multiplication factors come from using sideband transfers.

AGP Specification	AGP 1.0	AGP 2.0	AGP 3.0
Internal signaling	3.3 Volt	1.5 Volt	0.8 Volt
Peak speeds	1X = 266 MB/s 2X = 533 MB/s	2X = 533 MB/s 4X = 1066 MB/s	4X = 1.0 GB/s[1] 8X = 2.0 GB/s
Slot type	Keyed to back	Keyed to front or universal (both)	Keyed to front, same as 1.5 Volt

[1] *Rounding down from 1066MB/s.*

Aside from AGP speed, the factors affecting video card performance are the graphics processor and the amount of video RAM onboard. The minimum amount of RAM installed on an AGP adapter today is 8 MB, more than enough to display true color at the resolution a 17" monitors normally display. However, monitors and standard video adapters are designed to present two-dimensional images (2D). In the world of gaming, the illusion of three-dimensional (3D) space is key to a realistic experience. Video adapters with 3D graphics processors are essentially single-board computers and they need a lot of memory for texture maps and to support fast panning over an area larger than the display. You can get terrific 3D graphics out of a video adapter with 32 MB of RAM, but the trend is to add more and more, as much as 128 MB, to support 3D graphics on really big monitors. One of the penalties of adding RAM to a video card is increased power demand, requiring a bigger power supply and more cooling.

Case and Power Supply

Not long ago there was only one power supply standard for ATX PCs, which meant you could concentrate on *case geometry* (how many drive bays, front panel design) and not worry much about the power supply. All cases came with a 250-watt ATX supply and for a few bucks more you could upgrade it to 300 watts if you were loading up on drives. With the introduction of the power-hungry Athlon, AMD began certifying power supplies that could handle the load. Although the power supply connectors and power ratings were identical to regular ATX power supplies, they could be advertised as "for Athlon."

Then Intel introduced new Pentium 4 motherboards, which require a special 12-volt header (connector) on the power supply, in addition to the standard 20-wire connector. Some Pentium 4 motherboards can limp by without the presence of the extra connector, but it isn't recommended. Manufacturers implemented the additional power connector in two basic versions: a square four-pin connector, which is installed near the CPU or an old-fashioned six-pin inline connector such as the old AT power supplies, which attaches near the primary one. To make a long story short, if you are building a Pentium III, Celeron, or Duron, you can pretty much buy any old case and power supply that catches your eye (or your budget). But if you are building a Pentium 4 or Athlon, you'll need to purchase a case and power supply that is certified for the CPU.

Figure 2-8
A standard 20-wire connector and 4-wire 12-volt Pentium 4 connector

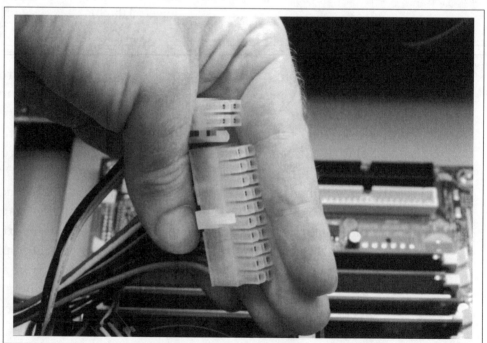

Moving beyond compatibility issues, the main figure of merit for a power supply is the power output, in watts. The minimum power supply sold these days is 250 watts, and that remains more than sufficient for any PC that isn't tricked out with an AGP Pro, a whole stack of drives, or top-end CPU. However, many cases now come standard with 300-watt supplies, and options all the way up to 450 watts are common. Buying more power supply than you need doesn't make a whole lot of sense, so unless you are installing some of the aforementioned power hogs, any case and power supply certified for the CPU should be fine.

Cases come in a number of sizes, shapes, and even colors. Sleek, space-age looks are becoming more popular, but be aware that you're paying for a lot of extra plastic that might interfere with ventilation. The same four basic models have been around 15 years, excluding the mini-ATX designs, which are not recommended for do-it-yourselfers. We build our P4 in a tower case, our Athlon/Duron in a midtower, and our Pentium III/Celeron in a minitower.

Case Type	Description	Drive Bays	Power Supply	Price
Minitower	Stands upright on desktop (12–18 inches high)	Two or three 5.25-inch bays, two or three 3.5-inch bays	250 watts	$30–$50 (Cases can be too stuffy for hot CPUs.)
Midtower	Stands upright on desktop or on floor (18–24 inches high)	Three or four 5.25-inch bays, three to six 3.5-inch bays	250–400 watts	$50–$100 (Top of the range for Athlon and Pentium 4 power supply.)
Desktop	Sits flat on desktop (6–8 inches high).	Two or three 5.25-inch bays, two or three 3.5-inch bays	250–300 watts	$35–$70 (These cases are going out of common use.)
Tower	Stands upright on floor (24–36 inches high)	Four or more 5.25-inch bays, three to eight 3.5-inch bays	300–450 watts	$100 on up. (Cases are heavy, but roomy to work in.)

Intelligent Drive Electronics (IDE)

One of the great innovations that appeared about 10 years ago was moving the brains of the hard drive from an add-in adapter out onto the hard drive itself. The primary and secondary IDE controllers integrated on your motherboard are really just bridges to the system bus. The *Basic Input/Output System* (BIOS), which handles all the low-level communications for the PC, works with a fictional picture of the actual hard drive geometry in terms of the number of heads, platters, and sectors—a sort of idealized pie chart with overlaying concentric rings. The intelligent electronics on the IDE hard drive translate these parameters, mapping them to the real geometry of the drive. In the case of CD and DVD drives and recorders, the data locations are measured in the time it would take to reach them playing the disc from the start at single speed, but the idea is the same. All the intelligence exists on the drive; hence IDE.

There are two IDE controllers built into every modern motherboard: the primary and secondary controllers. Each of these can be attached (by ribbon cable) to either one or two IDE drives. The standard arrangement is to install the boot hard drive as the "master" on the primary controller. Some PC builders like to install the CD/DVD as the "slave" on the primary controller to reduce the number of ribbon cables required. However, many of the IDE CD and DVD drives aren't quite as compliant with the standards as they should be. Overall, it's a safer bet to install these on the secondary controller, "master" for a single device or a "master/slave" combination for two. Recently, some motherboard manufacturers have begun offering an integrated IDE Redundant Array of Inexpensive Drives (RAID).

Until recently, RAID systems were very expensive and pretty much limited to network servers and other enterprise hardware. There are a dozen different levels of RAID implementation, but only three are supported by IDE controllers and practical for do-it-yourselfers. RAID arrays can offer two distinct advantages over an individual IDE drive: performance and reliability. The first RAID implementation, known as *RAID 0*, spreads your data over two or four IDE drives, which appear as single logical drive to the PC. This improves performance through striping reads and writes because the drives are appreciably slower than the controllers. Unfortunately, this increase comes at a loss of reliability, because if one drive fails, all your data is lost.

The second RAID implementation is known as *RAID 1*, and it writes all data to two drives, or two sets of drives, simultaneously. This creates a mirror image of all your data, so if one drive or set of drives fails, nothing is lost. RAID 1 offers a performance increase on reads but not on writes. RAID 10 (0+1) combines RAID 0 and RAID 1, giving you increased performance and reliability.

Figure 2-9
Adaptec RAID
controller

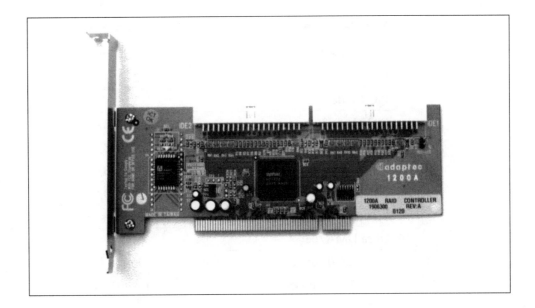

The original IDE interface was defined by the ATA (AT Attachment, as in
"PC AT") standard, adopted by the American National Standards Institute
(ANSI), and amounted to little more than some buffering between the system
I/O bus and the intelligent drive. When people refer to an ATA drive, they are
referring to an IDE drive; the terms are synonymous. The first improvement to
the original IDE standard, the *ATA Packet Interface* (ATAPI) extended the capability of the interface to work with CDs and other drives.

Many CDs and DVDs today are still labeled "ATAPI" devices, but again,
this just means they can be attached to an IDE controller. Performance enhancements included *Extended IDE* (EIDE) and *Fast ATA;* these were rolled
into the basic IDE standard. All new motherboards support all the transfer
types and speeds listed in the following table. The slower transfer modes use
Polled I/O (PIO), whereas the faster modes use *Direct Memory Access* (DMA),
reading the data directly from the cache memory on the drive into system
memory. Drives using the two fastest *Ultra DMA* (UDMA) modes must be attached with a special 80-conductor ribbon cable. This cable has the same
number of connectors as the standard 40-conductor ribbon cable, but includes a ground every other wire for noise shielding.

Transfer Type	Transfer Rate
PIO Mode 0	3.3 MB/s
PIO Mode 1	5.2 MB/s
PIO Mode 2	8.3 MB/s
PIO Mode 3	11.1 MB/s
PIO Mode 4	16.6 MB/s
DMA Mode 1	13.3 MB/s
DMA Mode 2	16.6 MB/s
Ultra DMA/33	33 MB/s
Ultra DMA/66	66 MB/s
UDMA/100 or ATA100	100 MB/s
ATA133 (proposed)	133 MB/s

Small Computer Systems Interface (SCSI)

The *Small Computer Systems Interface* is actually older than the IDE interface, and is still champion when it comes to connecting high-performance drives to servers and workstations. SCSI controllers take the opposite approach of the simple and inexpensive IDE controllers, by adding a whole new bus to the PC. With the exception of the cheapest SCSI (pronounced "scuzzy") adapters that occasionally shipped with scanners or other peripherals, original SCSI adapters could support up to seven devices, later this was increased to 15. This includes any combination of devices, hard drives, CD and DVD drives and recorders, proprietary optical drives, tape drives, scanners, and other peripherals both inside and outside the PC.

There are two types of internal cables in use with SCSI devices: the older 50-wire ribbon cable and the 68-wire *Low Voltage Differential* (LVD) ribbon cable. The LVD cable arranges all the wires in twisted pairs over which the differential (mirror image) signals are passed between the drives and controller.

Level	Known As	Number of Devices	Maximum Transfer Speed	Bus Width
SCSI-1	SCSI	7 (8 w/ controller)	5 MB/s	8 bits
SCSI-2	Fast SCSI	7	10 MB/s	8 bits
	Fast Wide SCSI	15 (16 w/ controller)	20 MB/s	16 bits
SCSI-3	Ultra SCSI	7	20 MB/s	8 bits
	Ultra-wide SCSI	15	40 MB/s	16 bits
	Ultra-2 SCSI	7	40 MB/s	8 bits
	Ultra 2 Wide SCSI or Ultra 80	15	80 MB/s	16 bits
	Ultra 3 SCSI	7	80 MB/s	8 bits
	Ultra 3 Wide SCSI or Ultra 160	15	160 MB/s	16 bits
SCSI 4 (expected in 2002)	Ultra 4 SCSI	15	320 MB/s	16 bits (support for 8-bit bus dropped)

Figure 2-10
LVD cable with terminator and 50-wire original SCSI cable

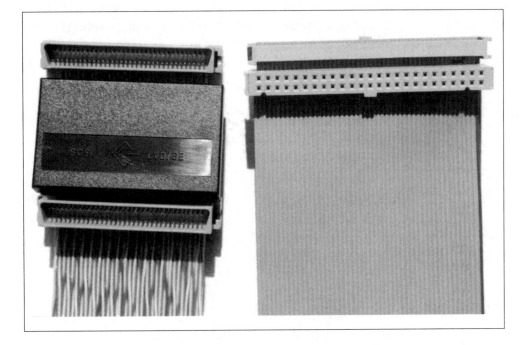

The SCSI bus is inherently more reliable than the IDE interface due in part to the large number of grounds in the ribbon cables to provide protection against electrical noise and cross-talk and because of termination. In order to eliminate signals reflecting back from devices at the ends of the bus,

SCSI buses have always required *termination*; installation of a dummy load to absorb any leftover power at the ends of the bus. External devices are either equipped with a switch to enable termination or a dummy load is attached to the open SCSI port of the last device on the chain.

Internal SCSI devices were traditionally equipped with either a jumper or a series of resistor packs that were removed when the device was not at the end of the bus (last device on the ribbon cable). Starting with Ultra 2 SCSI devices, the termination was moved onto the ribbon cable, and the devices shipped with termination disabled. Early SCSI controllers were also equipped with a jumper or switch to enable termination when they were on one end of the bus, and to disable termination if both internal and external devices were attached. Newer SCSI controllers give you the option to enable or disable termination in software.

Comparing Drive Performance

With the exception of floppy drives, which are all essentially the same, drive pricing is driven by capacity and performance. Capacity figures are easy enough to compare for hard drives and tape drives (CDs and DVDs are fixed capacity). The drive that holds the most gigabytes (GBs) wins. Whether you need all that storage and how much extra you are willing to pay for it is up to you, but for most people the performance is more important than the capacity, which is excessive to begin with.

Drive seek time is an average measure of how long it takes the drive to position the read/write head over a random location on the drive to begin reading or writing a file. This speed is measured in milliseconds (ms, thousandths of a second) and is usually less than 10 ms for hard drives. A similar measure exists for CD and DVD drives, but the seek times are five to ten times slower. Whereas the seek time was once considered the figure of merit when shopping for drives, it has been supplanted by the transfer rate for both hard drives and CD/DVDs, and the spindle speed for hard drives.

The transfer rate for hard drives is measured in MB/s, and just about all new IDE hard drives are rated as ATA100 or UDMA/100. This means that the IDE controller can use DMA to read or write the cache memory buffer on the hard drive at 100 MB/s. Given the relatively small size of the buffer, usually between 1–4 MB, and the relatively large size of many files, this isn't a terribly useful measure of hard drive performance. Somewhat more useful is the drive-to-buffer or buffer-to-drive rating, which falls well below the 100 MB/s mark for IDE drives or the 160 MB/s mark for the fastest SCSI drives.

Both the transfer measurements and the seek time are related to the spindle speed of the drive. The spindle speed is simply a measure of how fast the platters are spinning inside the drive. This is important because the faster they are spinning, the quicker any point on the drive comes under the read/write head and the faster the data can be streamed into the buffer of cache memory on the drive. For this reason, drives with higher spindle speeds, measured in *revolutions per minute* (RPM), also tend to have larger caches. The slowest IDE drives on the market today have a spindle speed of 4,500 RPM and the fastest run at 7,200 RPM. SCSI drives start off around 7,200 RPM and run as fast as 15,000 RPM, although 10,000 RPM is pretty much the standard for high performance.

CD and DVD drives are first and foremost rated by their *multiplier speed*, which describes how many times faster they are turning than the equivalent home entertainment system playing a music CD or movie. Single speed (1X) for CDs is defined as 150 KB/s; single speed for DVDs is 1,385 KB/s. Looking at the numbers for faster devices, a 50X CD reads data at 7.5 MB/s (7,500 KB/s) and a 2X DVD at 2.77 MB/s (2,770 KB/s). CD and DVD drives are much slower than hard drives and derive little benefit from being attached to fast interfaces.

CD recorders (CDRs) have three speeds associated with them, which are expressed, for example, as 16/10/40. The first number is the maximum write speed, the second is the maximum rewrite speed, and the third number is the maximum read speed. A fast write speed for CDRs is 16X, although 12X is still pretty good. A 16X CDR can record, or *burn*, an average length music CD (50 minutes) in about four minutes, including session information. Rewrite speeds are usually lower (and never greater) than write speeds, and in all cases the media you purchase must be rated at least as fast as the drive. The maximum read speed for CDRs is always a little slower than the maximum read speed for plain CD drives.

One commonly overlooked factor in purchasing a CDR is the recording software, most commonly Adaptec's Easy CD Creator. Do not buy a CDR without software unless you already own CDR software purchased as a shrink-wrap retail package. OEM software purchased with one CDR will not work with another brand. DVD-Rs are similar to the CDRs of five or more years ago, capable only of burning a permanent record with a laser on a die-coated disc. DVD-RAM (rewriteable) might be worth a look given the current high cost of both types of DVD blanks. Affordable DVD recorders were just entering the PC market at press time.

Drive Type	Capacity	Interface	Brand Names	Performance	Price Range
Hard drive	20–100 GB	IDE (ATA100)	Maxtor, IBM, Western Digital, Seagate	4,500–7,200 RPM. 1–4 MB cache	$75–$275, based on capacity and spindle RPM
Hard drive	10–180 GB	SCSI	Maxtor, IBM, Seagate	7,200–15,000 RPM. 4–16 MB cache	$175–$1,800, based on capacity and spindle RPM
CD drive	680 MB	IDE or SCSI	Mitsumi, Acer, Toshiba	44 X or higher	$30–$100, more for SCSI
CDR drive	680 MB	IDE, USB, SCSI	NEC, Toshiba, Matsushita, Ricoh, HP	16/12/40, write/rewrite/read	$60–$300, most for external SCSI
DVD drive	18 GB max (must eject to flip)	IDE, SCSI	Toshiba, Sony, Pioneer, Hitachi	40X reading CD, 6X reading DVD	$50–$150, more for movie decoder kit
DVD-R and DVD RAM Drives	4.7 GB	IDE, SCSI	Pioneer, Panasonic, Creative Labs	2X DVD-R, 1X DVD-RAM	$200–$800, depending on speed, interface
Tape drives, Travan or DAT	Travan 4–20 GB, DAT 4–240 GB	IDE, SCSI (oldest Travans used floppy)	Seagate, Exabyte, HP	Travan is slow, DAT 30 MB/minute–300 MB/minute	$150–$450 for Travan, $400–$5,000 for DAT
Cartridge Drives	Zip 100 MB or 250 MB, Jaz 2 GB	IDE, USB, SCSI	Iomega	Zip speed comparable to CD, Jaz to hard drive	$50–$150, 100 MB or 250 MB Zip, $250 for Jaz
Floppy Drive	1.44 MB, 120 MB Super Floppy (LS-120)	Floppy	LS-120, NEC, Imation, Mitsubishi	Slow	Floppy drive $10, LS-120 $50–$100

Modems

Modems are primarily used for connecting to the Internet, so we will approach them from that aspect. The original telephone modems worked by modulating an audio carrier frequency that could be transmitted through plain old telephone lines with a signal that could be decoded into binary data, 1s and 0s. To transmit and receive information, the device had to perform MOdulation and DEModulation, giving rise to the name MODEM. Early PC modems worked at 300 b/s and steadily improved, passing the fax speed of 9,600 b/s right up to 33 Kb/s (33,000 bits/second). There the technology hit the wall, and a new solution was needed.

The breakthrough was to dispense with the digital-to-analog conversion on the downstream side (from the Internet service provider [ISP] to your home) and transmit digital data. This technique can boost speed to 56 Kb/s, although you'll never see more than 53 KB/s in the United States because of

FCC regulations. Differences between competing standards were resolved several years ago, leaving us with the standard V.90 56 Kb/s modem.

In 2002, the V.90 standard will be replaced with V.92, which supports quicker connect times, call waiting, and faster uploads. However, it might be years before your ISP updates its modem pool to support the advanced features. Avoid purchasing a WinModem, a minimal hardware implementation that uses the CPU to do the signal processing work.

Even with the great advances in modem speed over the years, there remain a few problems that have brought alternative technologies into the market. The two primary issues are access and speed. Most people with 56 Kb/s modems won't see speeds much over 33 Kb/s on a sustained basis, unless their telephone infrastructure is in pretty good shape. Overloaded telephone infrastructure and ISP modem pools lead to frequent disconnects and busy signals. If you spend a lot of time online, you'll quickly tire of waiting for big chunks of information to download to your computer. Another problem is that the modem ties up your phone line, so you can't make or receive calls while online.

There are two mainstream alternatives to telephone modems: cable modems and *Digital Subscriber Line* (DSL) modems. Cable modems claim transfer rates as high as 43 Mb/s, and Asynchronous DSL (ASDL) modems as high as 8 Mb/s. Well, forget about ever seeing speeds that high. Real-world cable modem speeds run from the hundreds of kilobits per second to around 2 Mb/s, and consumer DSL packages steer clear of promising download speeds over 1.5 Mb/s, which costs extra.

The first consideration when it comes to choosing between cable and DSL is which (if either) is available to you. Not all cable companies offer cable modem access, and not all people live close enough to a telephone central office to get DSL. Another consideration, if both services are available to you, is package deals. Some cable Internet providers cut you a nice discount, providing you are already connected for cable TV; and some online services like AOL, have DSL arrangements with local telephone companies. In either case, if you are paying for an extra phone line for your PC, you can get rid of it, and the Internet connection will always be open, 24 hours a day.

Both cable and DSL are slower at uploading data from your PC to the Internet than downloading, but this isn't particularly important for most users. Two more modem technologies are *Integrated Services Digital Network* (ISDN) and satellite, but ISDN is being rapidly replaced by DSL and until I meet somebody with a satellite Internet connection, I'll pass on commenting.

When comparing prices, remember that cable and DSL services both replace your dial-up ISP, so if you were paying $21.95/month for dial-up, you can apply that money to the new bill. Don't run out and buy a cable or DSL modem before ordering the service! They might require you to purchase the modem through a particular retail chain or offer one for next to nothing as a signing bonus.

Modem Type	Requirements	PC Connection	Speed[1]	Costs
56 Kb/s modem	None, although if your ISP isn't in your area code, it gets expensive	Internal PCI modem or external serial port modem	53 Kb/s max in U.S. (by law), lower connection speeds normal	$20 Winmodem (software, avoid), $35–$50 fax/voice modem
Cable modem	Local cable carrier must offer service	10/100BaseT network adapter or USB	1–2 Mb/s download, 128–384 Kb/s upload	$200–$300, but don't buy before ordering service
DSL (Digital Subscriber Line)	Local telco must offer service, distance limitations	Usually a PCI adapter	1.5 Mb/s download, 384 Kb/s upload	Usually sold by the telco with the package for a nominal price

[1]*56 Kb/s modem speed depends greatly on local conditions. Cable modem speeds depend on how many people in your neighborhood are using the service, as the bandwidth is shared. DSL packages are priced at different points according to connection speed.*

Sound Cards

Most people want sound capability in home PCs, but only serious game players, musicians, and people attempting to replace their stereos need to look passed the most basic adapter. Many motherboards include basic sound capabilities at no extra cost, and an extremely capable PCI sound card can be purchased for $10. However, there is a high-end market that is focused as much on speakers as sound cards. The sound card market is dominated by Creative Labs, though Yamaha, ESS, and Diamond are also players. Higher-priced sound cards offer surround sound, 3D sound, four channels out (two speaker jacks), and high-quality A/D conversion (digital music recording from an external source). You can spend $100 on a sound card if you want, and the best way to see the latest, greatest offering is to pick up a PC magazine.

Network Adapters

As with sound capability, many motherboards now integrate 10/100BaseT network support. I am entirely brand blind when it comes to network adapters. The cheapest $10 adapter is fine by me. Network cards are the single exception to my "don't buy what you don't need now" rule, because the adapter that costs $10 from your mail-order parts vendor may cost $50 in a retail box. If you are purchasing a network adapter to connect to a cable modem, the story ends here, but if you are considering a home *Local Area Network* (LAN) to share resources, including Internet access, I would seriously consider going wireless. When you take into account the cost of 10/100BaseT cables, adapters, and a hub, you won't need to add much on top to go to a wireless LAN. Just don't confuse wireless home networking products (Ethernet) with wireless phone modems (cell phone accessories) when shopping online.

Figure 2-11
10/100BaseT
network adapter

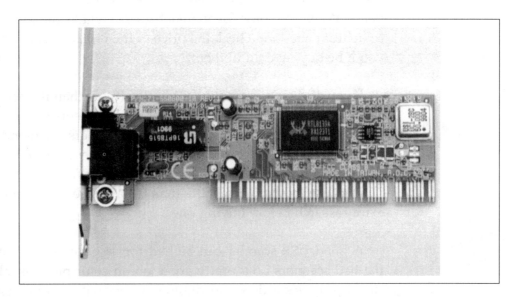

Video Monitors

Monitors have slowly gotten cheaper, so that 15" monitors are often sold for less than $100 and brand-name, flat-screen 17" monitors are available for $150 through mail order. A 15" LCD monitor is currently around $300, and large plasma screens used for presentation cost several thousand dollars. We went over the factors differentiating monitor quality in Chapter 1. LCD screens have an additional figure of merit, the viewing angle—the wider the better.

There is a pretty good correlation between brand name and quality for monitors, so be careful when buying an OEM or no-name brand. Often the hardware is identical to a name brand, but the final labor-intensive steps in quality control and focusing are skipped. You have two choices when it comes to buying a monitor: You can either walk into your local retailer and buy one off the shelf, hopefully on sale or with a rebate, or you can mail order one. As always, the main problem with mail order is shipping cost, which can run more than $30 for monitors. If there is a problem and you need to return it, your savings will evaporate in a hurry.

Printers and Scanners

Almost everyone will want to own a printer with his or her PC, and scanners are increasingly common purchases as their prices have fallen to less than $50. In short, a variety of color inkjet printers are available between $50–$200. Frequent replacement of the inkjet cartridges is a big hidden expense. When shopping for an inkjet, go to a retail store that will let you print some test pages and check the price of the replacement cartridges, because you'll be buying a lot of them.

If you do a serious amount of printing (more than 10 pages a day) and you can live without color, buy a laser printer. Excellent quality laser printers sell in the $300–$400 range. The more expensive lasers are intended for the really high-volume office environment, and the less expensive models have quality issues. Entry level color laser printers have fallen into the $1,000 range, but because they still cost more than the average PC, it's worth doing some extra research before buying one.

A good USB scanner can be had for as little as $30 with a rebate. All flat-bed scanners do a pretty good job on color pictures, although professional graphics artists and photographers will require something a little more upscale. If you are scanning pictures for the Internet or to e-mail to friends, use the lowest resolution available and save the image using *Joint Photography Experts Group* (JPEG) compression. Also, if you are buying a scanner specifically to do *Optical Character Recognition* (OCR), which is conversion of existing print documents into word processor files, make sure that the OCR software that comes with your scanner is a full version and not a 30-day trial.

Chapter 3

Before You Assemble Your PC

The following checklist should be completed when you order PC parts to make sure you have enough components to assemble a working PC:

❑ **ATX Case and power supply**   Note that both the Pentium 4 and Athlon have special power supply requirements, although many new power supplies provide for both of these.

❑ **ATX Motherboard and CPU**   Socket 421 or 478 for Pentium 4, depending on CPU model. Socket A for Athlon or Duron, Socket 370, or Slot 1 for Pentium III or Celeron.

❑ **RAM**   RIMM for Pentium 4, 128MB minimum (two pieces 64MB each), DDR for Athlon or Duron (DDR support for Pentium 4 is expected in early 2002), 64MB minimum, PC 133 for Pentium III/Celeron, 64MB minimum.

❑ **Video**   2X/4X AGP adapter with minimum 8MB video RAM (unless the motherboard has integrated video). Make sure the AGP adapter voltage is universal (3.3V or 1.5V) or matches your motherboard requirement.

❑ **Floppy drive**   1.44MB 3.5" floppy drive.

❑ **Hard drive**   20 GB IDE drive or larger, ATA 100 compatible with 80-conductor cable.

❑ **CD/DVD**   CD-ROM or CD recorder, DVD-ROM or combination CD-RW/DVD-ROM. Any of these can be used to install the operating system from CD.

❑ **Keyboard**   Keyboard with PS/2 style connector.

❏ **Mouse**   Mouse with PS/2 style connector.

❏ **Monitor**   15" or larger monitor.

❏ **Operating system**   Windows or Linux on CD, any version.

The following are optional but highly recommended and, with the exception of the speakers and power strip, might come integrated on the motherboard.

❏ **Modem**   56 Kb/s V.90 modem.

❏ **Sound card**   PCI sound card.

❏ **Network adapter**   10/100BaseT network adapter.

❏ **Speakers**   Speakers with separate power cord and adapter.

❏ **Switched power strip**   With surge protector.

Handling Parts and General Assembly Guidelines

Walking across a carpet can generate a static electric charge of 30,000 volts or more on your body. This is often manifested as a spark leaping from your hand to a doorknob or another person, creating a shock you both can feel. That same discharge, harmless to people (and doorknobs) because of the minute amount of electrical current involved, can ruin expensive computer components in a flash. Other activities that can generate static electricity include removing Styrofoam-encased parts from shipping boxes, taking off a jacket or sweater, or even sitting on a chair and gesturing during a conversation. That's the bad news.

The good news is that you can avoid building up a static electric charge, or at least zapping your components, by taking a few precautions. Most important, don't unpack your parts or assemble your PC in a room where you routinely receive static electric shocks. Next, get in the habit of frequently touching an electrical ground as you work. This ground can be a screw on the faceplate of an electrical outlet, a cold water pipe, or the metal casing of any electrical appliance or tool that uses a three-prong plug. If you plan to do a lot of PC work, it pays to pick up a $10 outlet tester at the local home improvement center to see if the grounds on your outlets are wired properly.

Make sure you keep your components in their static-proof shipping bags when you aren't handling them, and never pick up a component after crossing a room or wrestling with some packaging without grounding yourself first. If you have a damp basement in your home, this is the ideal place to assemble a PC, because humidity reduces static electric discharges.

If the neighborhood children flock to your house to chase each other around, sparks flying, you may consider the extra precautions of a grounding strap. Any decent electronics store will sell you a Velcro wristband with an inline 1 Megaohm resistor and an alligator clip that can be attached to the nearest ground. These are often recommended (or required) in the documentation that comes with your computer parts. The only drawbacks with grounding straps are that they are designed for sitting and working in one place, and they tend to breed overconfidence, making people forget the simple precautions against static discharge. There is also a danger of entanglement when working in an area cluttered with objects such as camera tripods and lights, which is why you won't see one in any of our assembly pictures.

Figure 3-1
Inexpensive
grounding strap

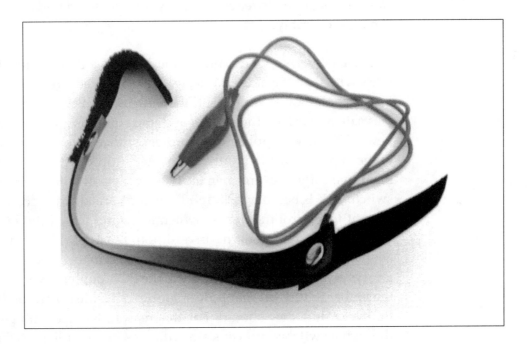

The other primary danger to your computer components, other than dropping them on the floor, is the electricity generated by your computer power supply. Computers are often powered up with the cover off when first assembled, just to make sure they work and that the front panel LED leads aren't connected to the motherboard backward. Even in the old days before ATX power supplies this was probably a bigger source of component damage than static electricity, as technicians and hobbyists alike would forget that the power supply was turned on and proceed to add or remove an adapter. This can cause power spikes and short circuits, which can easily damage adapters and motherboards.

Screws fumbled into the case while trying to secure an adapter in a "hot" system are another danger. Another dangerous scenario is when you drop a screw into the guts of the case during an assembly procedure and you use another screw to finish the job, intending to hunt down the escapee later. Never wait for later to retrieve a lost screw because it is just too easy to forget about it until it shows up jammed in just the wrong place under the motherboard, shorting out the whole system. Also, as a final check before powering up any newly built system, pick the whole case up and tilt it in every direction, listening for the telltale sound of a rolling screw. If you hear one, even if you can't get the sound to repeat, stop in your tracks and find it, even if it requires some disassembly.

ATX power supplies and motherboards, although generally easier to work with than the older AT design they replaced, create one new problem. With the old power supplies, if the switch was off and the fan was silent, it was safe to work on the system and you could use the case as ground. The new ATX power supplies are equipped with an override switch on the back of the supply to actually turn the power supply off, because the supply remains partially on even when the PC is turned off with the front panel power switch. This is because ATX motherboards are always receiving a trickle of current to control the power switch logic and afford the PC the ability to wake up on a preset alarm. In addition, to support the ability of network adapters and modems to wake the PC if activity occurs, a 720mA current is always available on the 5V supply to the PCI adapters. Not many people will remember to turn off that power supply override switch on the back of the PC every time they should. For this reason, I suggest plugging in the PC through a switched power strip with a switch that lights when it's on.

Finally, most power supplies are equipped with a recessed 115V/230V on the back of the power supply between the cord socket and the override switch. The voltage that shows is the voltage that is selected. Power supplies sold in the United States are usually set to 115V in the factory, but it pays to double check.

Figure 3-2
Voltage selector
switch

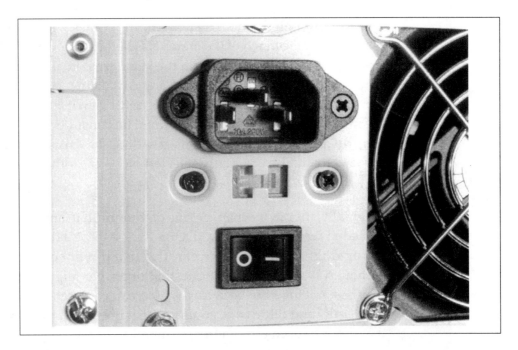

The only tool you absolutely need for assembling most PCs is a Phillips screwdriver. Nut drivers once came in handy for inserting brass standoffs to support the motherboard, but these have largely been replaced by permanent standoffs and various clip-in supports. Some manufacturers recommend using a nutdriver or screwdriver for levering down the heatsink clip, but I strongly advise doing it with your thumb if you can. If the tool should slip off the heatsink clip and smash into the motherboard, I doubt the warranty people will have a sense of humor about it. A large workspace isn't necessary, but a proven grounding point and good lighting are crucial, and a flashlight often comes in handy.

Before you begin to assemble your PC, look through all the pictures in this book (even the ones for the CPU types you aren't building) to become familiar with the steps involved. Your exact case might combine features from the different cases used here, and as chipset manufacturers provide new functionality for the motherboard makers, new combinations of memory types for the different CPUs are expected, such as DDR for the Pentium 4. Although each of the three systems tells a complete illustrated assembly story, we vary the order of the procedures and highlight certain features with each build. For example, our Pentium 4 is built with both SCSI and a IDE RAID disk subsystems, our Athlon/Duron has detailed finishing instructions for connecting peripherals and CMOS Setup, and our Pentium III/Celeron explores both Slot 1 and Socket 370 in addition to a very compact case.

Read through the documentation that comes with the all the parts you purchase. While much of the material is boilerplate, different manufacturers like to play different tricks with the standards. In all cases, the instructions that come with your parts trump any conflicting instructions in this book. For example, there is no standard for setting switches on the motherboard; the motherboard documentation must be consulted. It's also important to confirm that the switch and jumper setting shown as "default" in the motherboard manual are actually selected on your motherboard, because often they aren't.

Finally, the old mechanics' rule of thumb, "If it jams, force it—If it breaks, it needed replacing anyway" DOES NOT APPLY HERE. If your parts don't fit together nicely, make a careful visual inspection to find out why. Although it's usually just a question of proper alignment, it could well be they don't fit together because they were never intended to. It's better to feel a little silly and return one good part that doesn't fit than to return two parts that don't fit each other and are ruined to boot!

	Chapter 4	**Chapter 5**	**Chapter 6**
Case and power supply	Tower—300W w/ 12V for P4	Midtower—300W	Minitower—250W
CPU and socket	2.0 GHz Intel Pentium 4, Socket 478	AMD Athlon/Duron, Socket A	Intel Pentium III/ Celeron, Slot 1/ Socket 370
Motherboard features	Sound, 10/100BaseT network, USB ports and hub, ATA 100, AGP 4X support	USB, ATA 100, DDR memory support, AGP 4X support	AGP video adapter, sound, 10BaseT network, 56Kb/s modem
RAM installed	256MB RIMM	256MB DDR	64MB PC133
Highlights	Adaptec 160MB/s SCSI and IDE RAID, USB 2.0 adapter	Vanilla system, CMOS Setup detail, and peripheral connections	Hinged power supply, adapter risers, very inexpensive

Problems to Watch Out For

Five basic things can go wrong before or during PC assembly that will prevent it from powering up and operating properly:

❏ **Faulty connections** This is the most common problem, and it includes improperly made ribbon cable connections to the drives or motherboard; switch, fan, and LED connections partially made or connected to the wrong points on the motherboard; partially inserted power connectors; poorly seated CPUs and memory modules; improperly installed heatsinks; and adapter cards not fully seated in the bus connectors. Illustrations follow this discussion.

❏ **Improper settings**   These can be jumpers or switches on the motherboard, the voltage switch on the power supply, or software settings made in CMOS Setup after the initial power up. The wrong voltage selection on the power supply (115V or 230V) will ruin components, as can an improper CPU voltage. Improper settings in CMOS Setup will generally result in resource conflicts, poor performance, or inconsistent behavior and lockups. In all instances, the only source for motherboard settings is the small manual that ships with the motherboard or the settings printed on the motherboard itself. Most new motherboards can automatically select all the proper manufacturer recommended settings for the CPU and are sold with this option selected as the default, but always double-check the actual settings against the manual.

❏ **DOA (Dead On Arrival) parts**   Although this problem is less common than generally thought, especially given the poor packaging used by many mail-order vendors and incredibly low component pricing, you might encounter a DOA component. Troubleshooting which component is dead often requires access to a working PC to swap out parts (see Chapter 8). This is the best reason to buy your motherboard, CPU, RAM, case, and video adapter (the minimum needed to get a live screen) from the same vendor to simplify return issues.

❏ **Incompatible or poorly selected components**   This is rare with the motivated do-it-yourselfer, but a careless selection of parts from an Internet site may leave you with a Slot 1 CPU for a Socket 370 motherboard or a Pentium 4 that doesn't match the socket. The best way to avoid this type of problem is to keep a written list of selected parts and their requirements as you shop, and not make snap decisions on attractively priced components.

❏ **Carelessness**   Dropping parts, leaving loose screws rattling around the case, wearing a wool sweater and pulling it off over your long hair and then picking up the CPU without grounding yourself... all these things happen. The only antidote for carelessness is staying alert, but not by drinking a coffee over your open PC!

Faulty Connections

The most common mistake of new PC builders is not making sure adapter cards are properly seated in the slots before closing the case. Even if the adapter seats properly when you initially push it into the slot, it may pop partially out again when another adapter is seated in an adjacent slot. Paradoxically, the leading reason for PCI and AGP adapters to pop out of their slots is the insertion of the screw that is intended to hold them in place. This happens because the PCI slots, and even more the AGP slot, are located farther from the back of the case than the original ISA slots were. When the screw forces down the port end of the adapter, it might pivot on the back edge of the slot causing the front edge of the adapter to lever partially out of position. Some of the newer AGP video adapters and slots are designed with a retention mechanism to prevent just this failure.

Figure 3-3
PCI adapter
partially out
of the slot

A similar result often occurs when memory modules are inserted unevenly. This is why we emphasize seating a module with two thumbs and letting the white locking levers at the ends of the memory slots raise into place on their own as the module is properly seated. Wedging the module in on one end first and pulling up on the locking levers to encourage it into place can damage the memory slot or result in a failed insertion.

Figure 3-4
Partially seated
DIMM

The most likely reason for a system to fail to power up once it's plugged in and the switch is pressed on the front panel is that the power switch lead is attached to the motherboard improperly. This can result from a mistake in reading the motherboard manual or on-board markings, but it can also occur simply because the connection block for panel leads is dense with tightly spaced posts. Squinting through a maze of wires in a poorly lit work area can lead to all sorts of missed connections. The power switch, a two-lead connector, is shown below with only one half of the connector on a post.

Figure 3-5
Power switch
missing the post

All the new CPUs are keyed so they can only be inserted in the proper ori-entation, but partial insertion is still a possibility with them all. This is more common with the older CPU types such as the Slot A Athlon and the Slot 1 Pentium III, because the edge connectors rely on spring force to make good contact with the processor cartridges, and therefore require strong pressure to insert and seat fully. Normally, when a slot-type system is powered up with a partially seated CPU, the power LED comes on, the drives whir, but the screen remains dead. Socket CPUs can also be partially inserted, usually due to being pushed into place with the locking lever not completely open or through sheer carelessness. The lever can be closed with the CPU cocked at an angle and, in some cases, the heat sink can even be locked in place over it.

Figure 3-6
Failed CPU insertion

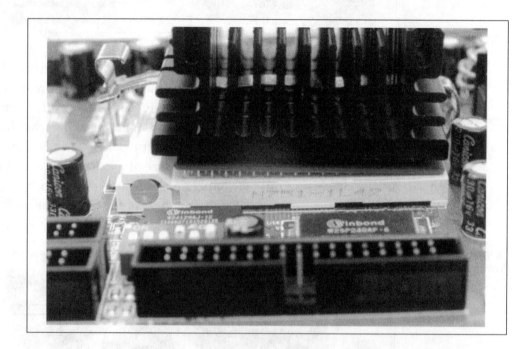

The most problematic drive connection is always the floppy drive. The connectors on the drives are only rarely boxed and keyed, and sometimes labeling for the pin 1 end of the connector is hard to find. The ribbon cables can be put on backward, forced on missing a full row of the two rows of pins, or even missing one set of pins at one of the ends of the connector. Some floppy cabling problems are immediately apparent because the small LED on the front of the drive stays permanently lit once the system is powered up.

If you encounter floppy drive problems, undo and remake the connection, even if you have to remove the drive again to get a good look at it. The hardest cabling problem to spot is when two pins on the down end miss the connector and are bent out of the way. When the cable is removed, the pins will still appear straight if you sight down the rows, and the connector will continue to mate improperly until you notice the bent pins and bend them back.

Figure 3-7
Floppy ribbon
cable connector
missing two
pins on end

Ribbon cables also are prone to failure when poorly constructed or removed and remade a number of times. This is due to the lack of a large plastic header on the cable, which forces you to pull on the ribbon cable itself if you want to undo the connection. If the snaps fail on a connector header and it begins to fall apart, don't even think about pressing it back together, just get a new one.

Figure 3-8
Ribbon cable
connector failure

One last problem that deserves mention, although it is not a traditional connector issue, is using the wrong screws in the wrong places. This simple mechanical issue can lead to stripped threads, dangerous metal flakes, and endless frustration. There are three types of screws used in most computers, not including variations in head design. Fine thread screws are used for floppy drives and CD/DVD drives, and on rare occasions for motherboard installation and adapter hold down screws. The thinner of the coarse thread screws are used for hard drives, mounting motherboards, adapter hold downs, and case cover screws. The fatter coarse thread screws are not found in many PCs, but when they are, they are used exclusively for case cover screws.

Figure 3-9
Three types
of screws

Chapter 4

Building a Pentium 4 in a Tower Case

Step 1: Preparing the Case

We chose to build our Pentium 4 in a tower case to better illustrate the IDE RAID and SCSI disk subsystems we include as options. Tower cases tend to be top heavy, so they are often constructed with fold-out feet on the bottom for stability. This tower case features a drive access door that can be locked, a handy feature for a classroom server.

Figure 4-1
Tower case

There are two basic varieties of tower and midtower case designs. The sides, or lids of this tower, are secured with two screws at the back of the case and the front facade is never removed. The other approach is to hide all the screws under the front facade, as in our Athlon/Duron build. To open the case, begin by removing the screws from the top lid, which is the left side of any tower or midtower PC.

Figure 4-2
Removing the screw securing the case lid

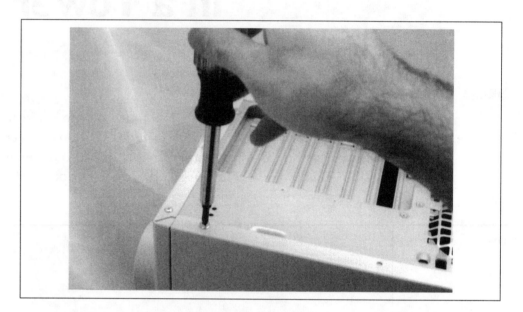

Another feature of this tower case is the lockable release handle on the lid. Even after the screws are taken out, if the release handle is locked, the lid can't be removed. Security features are common on tower cases, which tend to be loaded with expensive components and "easy out" designs for mounting the drives. The release is pushed in and the lid is lifted away from the case.

Figure 4-3
Releasing the lid

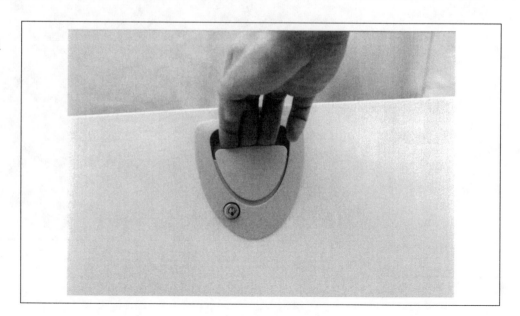

One of the benefits of buying an upscale case is the engineering design. The tower came stock with two exhaust fans (bottom right) and provides snap-in installation for up to two intake fans at the front. The 5.25" drive bays all employ rails, which are stored in holders on the bottom of the case. The screws and other hardware are taped in place between the rail holders.

Figure 4-4
Tower case
features

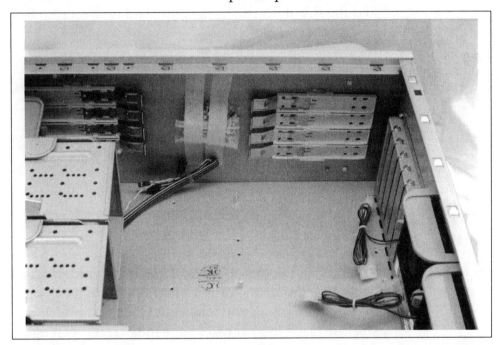

The Intel D850MD motherboard we are installing is shipped with its own I/O shield. The standard I/O shield with which all cases ship is equipped with punch-outs that will match the majority of motherboard I/O cores, but the five USB ports in our motherboard I/O core exceed the standard design. The first step is to remove the stock I/O shield by pushing it into the case. You might need to pry with a flat-bladed screwdriver to get it started.

Figure 4-5
Popping out
the stock I/O
core shield

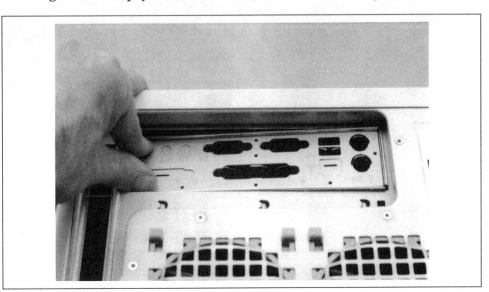

The new I/O shield is installed from the inside of the case. The smooth side of the I/O shield, which is stamped with symbols describing port functions, faces out through the opening. The inward side of the I/O shield is identified by the springy metal tabs for grounding the ports to the case. The two circular holes, one above the other, are the keyboard and mouse ports, and the shield is installed so these end up closest to the power supply.

Figure 4-6
Positioning the
new I/O shield

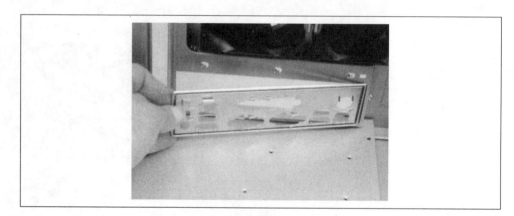

Once the shield is in place, it's snapped into position by pushing at the edges from inside the case. The shield is designed with the edges doubled over and projecting outward, providing a natural spring effect to hold the shield in place. In some cases the standard I/O opening is a little oversized so the shield doesn't want to stay in place, but once the motherboard is installed it will be locked in.

Figure 4-7
New I/O shield
snapped into
place from inside
the case

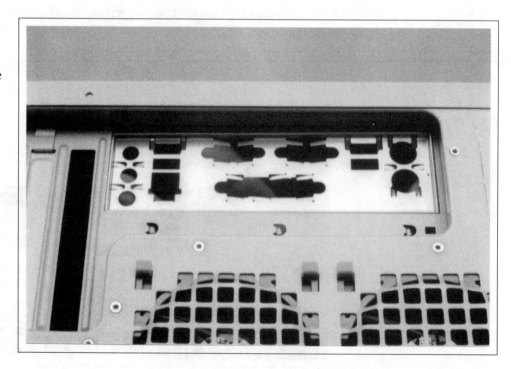

We purchased one additional case fan, commonly called a *muffin fan* to draw air into the case through the front facade vents. Muffin fans draw air in the direction of the label on the motor, and this fan will complement the two exhaust fans on the back of the tower. When adding fans to a case, it's important to establish an airflow direction, usually front to back, and make sure all fans move the air in the same direction, rather than fighting each other.

Figure 4-8
Muffin fan

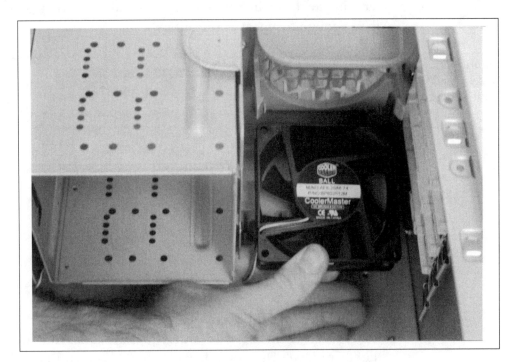

The fan is installed in this case simply by snapping it into place. The through holes in the four corners of the muffin fan align with pegs in the holder, and the two plastic retainers snap over the fan body. This is a tremendous improvement over cases that require you to mount any additional fans with four slender bolts or long plastic rivets. The bolts or rivets are rarely supplied with either the case or the fan, which forces you to run to a hardware store to continue.

Figure 4-9
Snapping the
muffin fan
in place

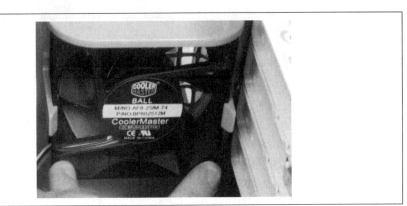

Step 2: Installing CPU and Heatsink

The motherboard in this build is the first to support the 2.0 GHz Pentium 4 in Socket 478. It features dual-channel RDRAM support, integrated audio, 10/100 BaseT networking, and five USB ports. The micro ATX layout only supports three PCI expansion slots (the vertical white slots to the bottom left), but with the integrated features and all those USB ports, that's more than enough for most applications.

Figure 4-10
Intel D850MD
motherboard

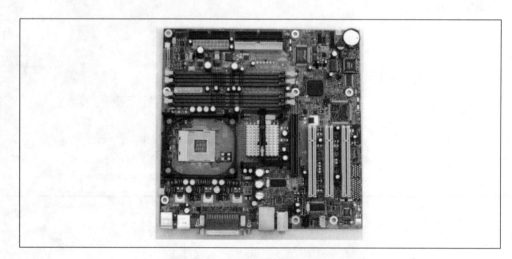

The Pentium 4 for Socket 478 is physically smaller than any of the other CPUs currently in use, due largely to the smaller dimensions employed on the silicon level. The chip is keyed to the socket with a missing pin in one corner, so it can't be inserted the wrong way.

Figure 4-11
Pentium 4 keyed
to Socket 478

The first step to install the CPU is to lift the locking lever on the side of the socket. Move the lever a little away from the side of the socket to free it from the hold-down, and gently pull it up until it stops. It shouldn't require any force to move the locking lever. You can actually lift it with one finger once it's past the hold-down.

Figure 4-12
Lifting the
locking lever

The Pentium 4 is placed in the socket with the keyed corner, also marked by the black dot, matching the socket key. The locking lever is lowered back into the tuck position. Don't be surprised by the great change in resistance between raising the lever and lowering it. The lever locks 478 pins in place by spring force.

Figure 4-13
Locking the
Pentium 4
in place

The Pentium 4 heatsink for Socket 478 actually consists of three pieces. The first of these, the retention module, came permanently mounted on the motherboard. The two pieces shown here are the retention clip and the active heatsink, a fan mounted on a finned aluminum structure that maximizes surface area to disperse the heat.

Figure 4-14
Active heatsink and retention clip

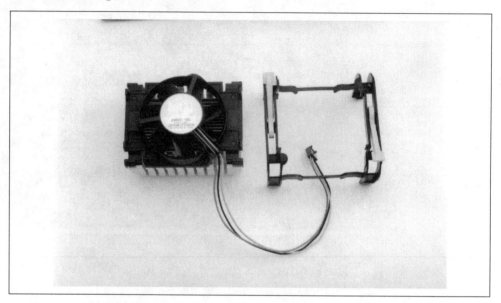

The dark area on the bottom of the heatsink is a pre-applied thermal interface, saving us from the need to apply thermal grease to the CPU package. The retention clip is placed over the heatsink and the whole assembly is lowered into the retention module. The heatsink settles over the CPU, held a slight distance above it by the pads in the corners of the retention module.

Figure 4-15
Lowering the heatsink and retention clip into place

The retention clip fits loosely over the heatsink, with its four clips lined up with the four holes in the retention module posts. Push the whole retention mechanism down over the heatsink to lock the individual clips in place. These clips make an audible "click" as they are pushed over the retention module, but the whole assembly sits quite loosely.

Figure 4-16
Seating the retention clip over the heatsink and retention module

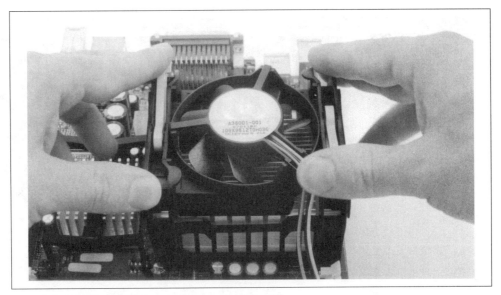

The two levers that force the heatsink into contact with the CPU and lock the whole assembly into place actually move in opposite directions. Lift both levers (I do this simultaneously) and bring them all the way over until they lock down in the opposite positions. This takes even more force than the locking lever on the CPU socket.

Figure 4-17
Locking the heatsink assembly into place

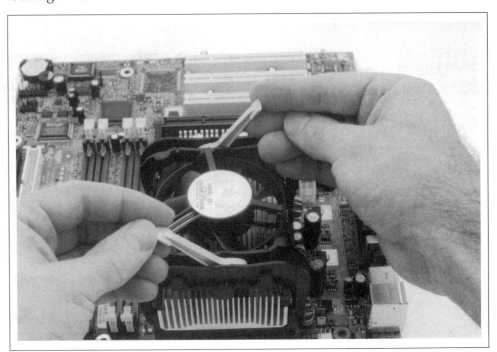

As soon as the active heatsink is locked in place, attach the fan to the CPU fan point on the motherboard, normally labeled "fan 1." This allows the motherboard BIOS (Basic Input/Output System) to monitor the CPU fan speed and manage it in power saver and sleep modes. In this instance, the fan 1 connector was the closest connector to the CPU socket, but this isn't always the case, so check your motherboard documentation.

Figure 4-18
Connecting
the CPU fan

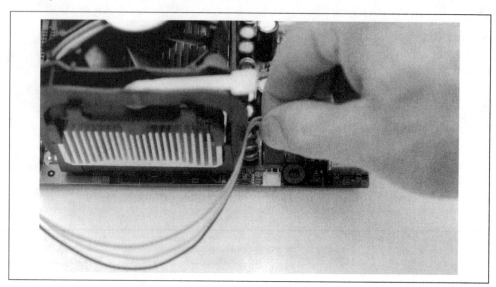

Step 3: Installing Memory

The D850MD motherboard supports two banks of RDRAM for a total of up to 2 GB of memory. We are installing two pieces of 128 MB RDRAM for a total of 256 MB. The RIMM modules are keyed with two notches so they can't be installed backward.

Figure 4-19
128 MB Kingston
RIMM over
RDRAM socket

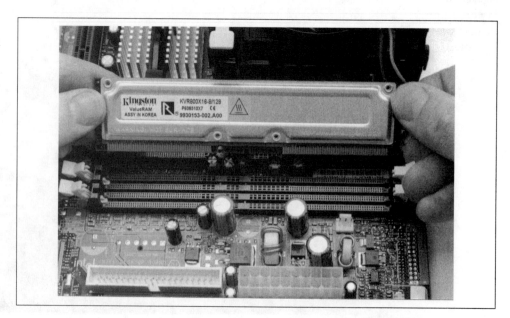

Before installing any modules, make sure the white locking levers on the sides of the sockets are spread. As you seat the module by applying even pressure with two thumbs, the white levers will raise into position. This requires a good deal of pressure, so do this with the motherboard placed on its static bag on a hard, flat surface.

Figure 4-20
Seating the
first RIMM

The second RIMM is installed in the same bank as the first, filling Bank 0 before Bank 1. RIMM modules are only 8 bits wide, so it takes two modules to make up the 16-bit dual-channel memory bus width. The metal covers of the RIMMs carry a warning to not touch them when the computer has been running, because they get very hot.

Figure 4-21
Seating the
second RIMM

The RDRAM architecture requires that all empty sockets be filled with CRIMMs, empty circuit boards that provide continuity to the bus. The CRIMMs are aligned with two notches, the same as the RIMMs. Make sure the locking levers are spread, and seat the CRIMMs with even pressure from two thumbs. If you prefer to install your memory modules with the motherboard in the case, make sure there is sufficient support under the memory socket area to bear the load of the insertion force.

Figure 4-22
CRIMM
over socket

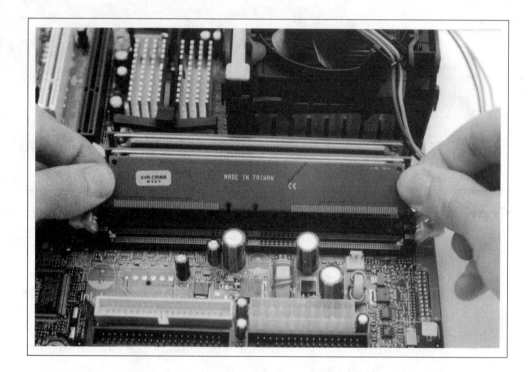

Our two RIMMs are installed in Bank 0 and our two CRIMMs are installed in Bank 1. This motherboard is entirely jumperless, meaning that the CPU and memory configuration is automatic. See the Athlon/Duron build for an example of manual selection of memory bus speed. See the Pentium III/Celeron build for manual selection of CPU socket. In all instances, check the motherboard manual for any settings, and make sure the defaults are actually selected on your motherboard.

Figure 4-23
Completed
memory
installation

Step 4: Installing the Motherboard

The next step is to test fit the motherboard in the case. Use two hands to hold the motherboard over any existing standoffs and check the fit with the I/O shield. Next, count the number of silver rimmed holes in the motherboard that line up with holes in the case (all of them should). Set the motherboard off to the side on its static bag and remove any standoffs that don't line up with the holes in your board.

Figure 4-24
Test fitting the
motherboard

Install standoffs in the case holes that match your motherboard. Do not use standoffs that ship with the motherboard unless you remove all the standoffs that are installed in the case. Slight differences in standoff height can put unacceptable stress on the motherboard. The standoffs that shipped with this case are the standard brass type, which can be tightened with a nut driver or pliers, but don't over tighten or they may break.

Figure 4-25
Installing a brass standoff

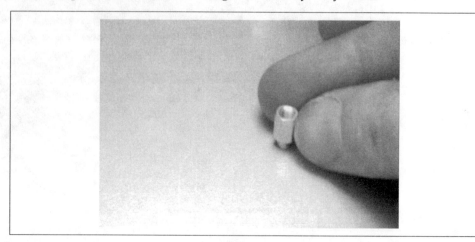

Count the number of standoffs installed and set aside that number of screws. Reinstall the motherboard in the case, securing the corners first. It's usually best to start with the corner by the memory sockets, across from the I/O core. The little tabs on the I/O shield can apply enough spring force that you need to really keep the motherboard pushed into the shield as you install the screw. Secure the other corners, and then fill in the other screws. If you finish with one of your set-aside screws left over, remove the motherboard and takeout the standoff that didn't line up with a hole.

Figure 4-26
Installing a motherboard screw

Here you can see the I/O core of the installed motherboard properly aligned with the I/O shield. Above the I/O core are the two exhaust fans. The airflow direction can be confirmed by noting that the labels on the fan motors are visible through the grate.

Figure 4-27
I/O core aligned
with I/O shield

The next step is to attach the main ATX power connector to the motherboard. The 20-wire connector is keyed so that it can only be installed one way, and it is automatically secured by the plastic spring latch. The power supply should not be plugged in or switched on until the build is complete.

Figure 4-28
Attaching the ATX
power connector

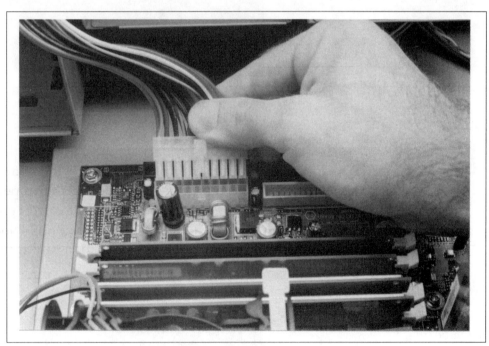

With the introduction of the Pentium 4, Intel required an additional 12 V lead from the power supply to the motherboard. Some P4 motherboards use an old-fashioned AT power connector to supply additional power for the CPU or AGP Pro slot, but none of our builds use one of these. We attach the 4-wire 12V power connector next to the I/O core.

Figure 4-29
Attaching the
12 V header

The muffin fan that we previously installed in the front of the case needs a power connection, and one is conveniently located nearby on the corner of the motherboard. Using the motherboard connection means the computer can monitor the fan status. The muffin fan in our Athlon/Duron build is powered directly from a power supply lead.

Figure 4-30
Attaching the
muffin fan
power lead

The most important of the front panel leads to the motherboard is the power switch. This two-wire connector can go on the proper two posts either way, unlike LEDs, which will only work with the correct polarity. The circular unit below and slightly to the left of the connection block is an onboard piezoelectric speaker, eliminating the need for a case speaker connection.

Figure 4-31
Attaching the
power lead to the
motherboard

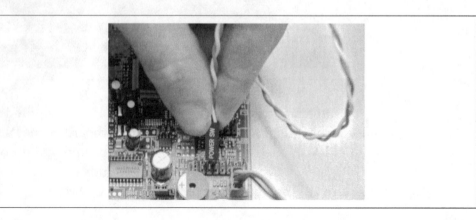

Step 5: Installing Adapters

We install our 4X video adapter with 32 MB of video memory in the single AGP slot. This 3D AGP Phantom from MSI is nearly identical to the nVIDIA Sniper II used in the Athlon/Duron build, as both use the same video accelerator. However, the software that ships with the card is different, and this makes a great deal of difference in terms of how it is utilized in Windows.

Figure 4-32
Installing the
AGP adapter

Secure the adapter with a screw on the back rail immediately after installation. Make sure the front edge of the adapter doesn't come out of the AGP slot as the back edge is forced down by the screw. Note that the PCI slot next to any video adapter with a heatsink on the video processor is nearly useless. Even though you can fit an adapter in, it will be too close to the heatsink to allow for decent air circulation.

Figure 4-33
Securing the
AGP adapter

Planning and foresight can save you a lot of wasted steps when you build a PC. We know we will be installing a DVD at a later point, and we know that the motherboard has integrated sound. For the DVD to play music CDs, the stereo lead must be connected to the proper point on the sound card or, in this case, motherboard. Because that point happens to be between the PCI slots, we take the time to do it right now.

Figure 4-34
Attaching the stereo lead for the DVD

The 56 Kb/s modem is installed in the second PCI slot, a safe distance from the heatsink on the video card. For our basic build, these are the only two adapters we need to install because all the other features we want are integrated on the motherboard. The adapter is jumperless and all the settings are handled from within Windows.

Figure 4-35
Installing the modem

There are two tricks to installing any adapter with recessed ports. The first trick is to make sure the ports actually line up with the slot in the back of the case so that the connectors, telephone jacks in this case, can be inserted and removed. The second trick is getting the screw into the adapter when the rail is recessed under the edge of the case. All the pictures in this book show the screw being tightened by a screwdriver, but I usually start them by hand.

Figure 4-36
Starting the modem hold-down screw

Step 6: Installing the Drives

The reason for choosing this tower case is the elegant construction of the drive cages. Because we will be illustrating IDE RAID and SCSI options on this system in later steps, we'll be replacing and removing many hard drives. The first step is usually to install the floppy drive and boot hard drive in the top cage. The cage is secured by a simple locking lever, pulled back here by the thumb.

Figure 4-37
Removing the
drive cage

There are so many possible mounting locations for the floppy drive in this cage that we need to do a test fitting. The first step is to remove the metal RF shield blocking the floppy port. These are held in place by metal tabs that are broken by wiggling the shield back and forth. In some instances you may have to remove both shields to get the floppy drive aligned with the opening in the front facade.

Figure 4-38
Removing the
metal RF shield

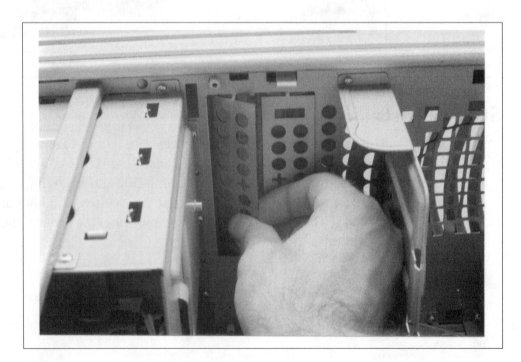

The white plastic blank on the front facade blocking the opening is popped out from behind with the fingers. Now you can replace the cage in its position and lock it in place. Slide the floppy drive in from the front until the faceplate is flush with the facade; then insert a single screw to hold it in that position.

Figure 4-39
Finding the correct floppy drive position

Remove the cage and secure the floppy drive with three more fine-thread screws. Some PC builders have abandoned floppy drives altogether because most software is delivered on CD or over the Internet. Floppy drives do have many problems, as we detailed in the introductory chapters, but for the extra $10, it's worth installing one.

Figure 4-40
Securing the floppy with four fine-thread screws

Next we install the hard drive in the bottom of the cage. The 80 GB Maxtor drive could have been installed in the middle of the cage, but it's always a good idea to put as much space as possible between drives. The connectors must face into the case, and I always install hard drives so they will run upside up, even though the manufacturers claim they are just as happy upside down.

Figure 4-41
Securing the hard drive with four coarse screws

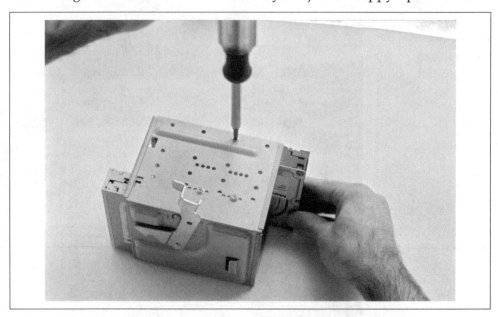

The cage is slid back into the case with the drives installed. Even though we lined up the floppy drive with the opening, it might take some jiggling to get it in, and you might have to remove the metal RF shield for the other 3.5" opening. As soon as the cage is installed, lock it into place with the lever. Otherwise, it can come sliding out when you stand up the case and crash into the motherboard.

Figure 4-42
Installing the loaded drive cage

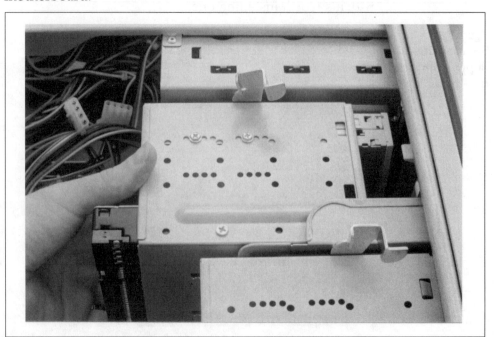

The 5.25" drives in this tower are rail mounted. Proper rail position is determined by experimentation, but they normally mount as far forward as they can go with the rail positioned as close to the bottom of the drive as possible. Even when doing a trial fit, attach both rails with two fine-thread screws each, and if you guess right, you're done.

Figure 4-43
Installing rails
on the DVD drive

Pop the plastic bay cover out from inside the case in the bay without the RF shield. Case manufacturers assume that every PC will be built with at least one 5.25" drive, so one bay is left unshielded. Slide the drive slowly into the case, stopping if it binds. A common mistake is to position the rails differently on the two sides of the drive. When the drive settles in place, you shouldn't be able to push it out from the back without depressing the spring clips from the front.

Figure 4-44
Installing the
DVD drive

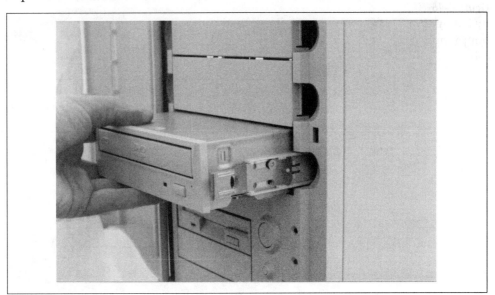

Step 7: Connecting the Drives

There is no rule for the order in which drive connections should be made, as long as they are made correctly. We begin here with the floppy ribbon cable connection to the motherboard. The connector is usually keyed, but you should still double-check that the red key wire in the cable is oriented to the pin 1 end of the connector, often marked with an arrow.

Figure 4-45
Connecting the floppy ribbon cable to motherboard

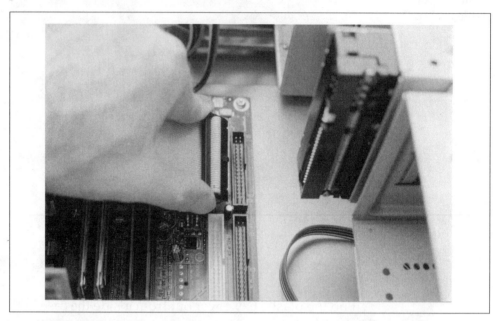

The connector on the other end of the ribbon cable is connected to the back of the floppy drive with the red key wire again toward pin 1 on the drive. This ribbon cable connection is probably the most problematic connection in building a PC. The cable can be forced on missing an entire row of pins, as detailed in Chapter 3.

Figure 4-46
Installing the floppy ribbon cable

The small format power connector also causes more problems than any other power connector in the system. There is a rectangular indent on one side of the connector that matches a rectangular tab under the four pins on the drive. The protruding ridge visible on the side of the connector shown here should prevent the connector from being installed upside down, but it pays to take a good look at the drive if it doesn't fit on easily.

Figure 4-47
Connecting power to the floppy drive

Connect the blue header on the 80-conductor ribbon cable to the primary IDE controller on the motherboard. The connection is keyed to fit one way only. One of the advantages of buying a hard drive in a retail pack is you are sure to get a quality 80-conductor ribbon cable. When you see that the hard drive is close to the motherboard connection, you can fold up the slack in the cable and catch it with a cable clamp, tie-wrap, or, failing all else, a thin rubber band.

Figure 4-48
Attaching the ribbon cable to the primary IDE controller

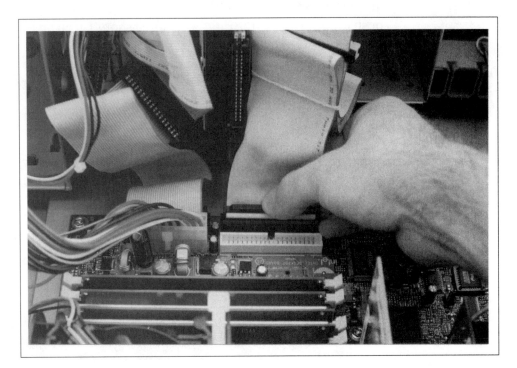

The master drive on a high-speed IDE controller (ATA100 or ATA66) must be attached to the far end of the 80-conductor ribbon cable using the black connector. The connection is keyed to work one way only, but you can double-check that the red key wire is toward the power connector. For an illustration of a master/slave arrangement on one controller, see the Pentium III/Celeron build.

Figure 4-49
Connecting the ribbon cable to the hard drive

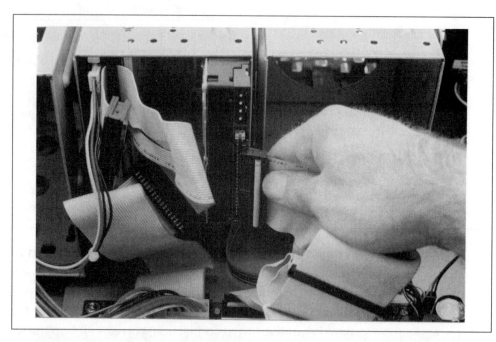

The large format connector used for hard drives and CD/DVDs can only be inserted one way thanks to two angle-cut corners. The connector might not push in all the way to the ridge stop, but it should go in far enough that it doesn't pull out easily.

Figure 4-50
Connecting power to the hard drive

The most overlooked connection in PC assembly is the stereo lead from the CD/DVD, without which you can't play music CDs on your PC. This has nothing to do with the sound used in PC games or the operating system, so a PC is often in use for a long time before somebody tries to play a CD and realizes something is wrong. The lead is sold with the CD or DVD; it should even be included with "bare" drives. This is the other end of the cable we connected between the PCI slots.

Figure 4-51
Connecting the stereo lead to the DVD

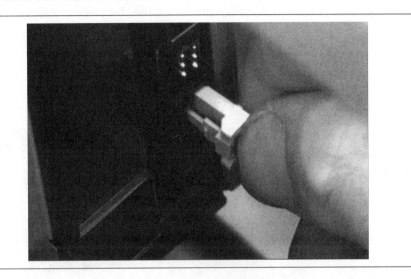

We connect the ribbon cable for the DVD to the secondary IDE controller on the motherboard and to the back of the drive, just like we did with the hard drive. For a really exhaustive treatment of drive connections, see the Athlon/Duron build. Due to the large number of drive connections coming up in our IDE RAID and SCSI options, we'll skip forward to connecting the power lead to the DVD.

Figure 4-52
Connecting power to the DVD

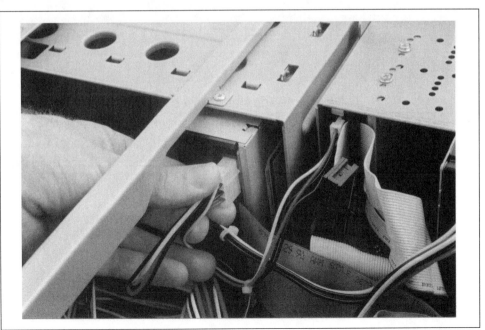

At this point our basic Pentium 4 build is finished, and you can skip to step 8.

Option 1: An IDE RAID

We install our Adaptec 1200A RAID controller in the open PCI slot. The adapter is jumperless, but it comes with its own BIOS, just like the motherboard. This software is reached by pressing CTRL+H while the system is starting and provides the basic array configuration. The subject of configuring and managing arrays is beyond the scope of this book; the controller ships with its own 68-page booklet.

Figure 4-53
Installing the
Adaptec RAID
controller

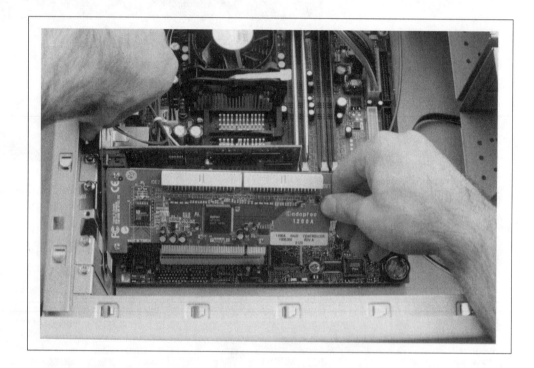

Secure the adapter with a screw. Note that if you connect the hard drive activity LED that normally connects to the motherboard to the adapter, it will only show activity when the RAID drives are being accessed. In addition to the BIOS software, the adapter ships with operating system drivers on CD, which also must be installed.

Figure 4-54
Securing the
RAID controller

We will build a two-drive RAID 1 array that employs mirroring for data security. We begin by attaching the 80-wire ribbon cable to the IDE 1 connector. The blue connector goes to the controller and the black to the drive, just as if it were being attached to the motherboard.

Figure 4-55
Attaching the
ribbon cable to the
IDE 1 connector

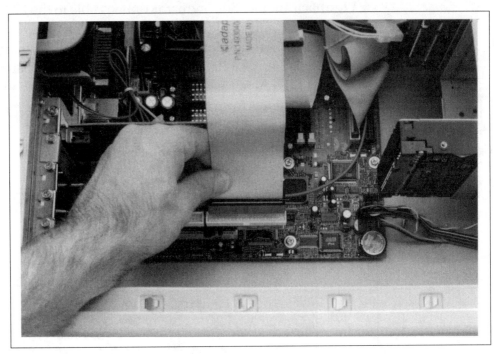

As we connect the ribbon cable to the hard drive that was the boot drive in our basic build, you can see that we have installed another identical hard drive in the second cage. Pairs of hard drives in RAIDs must be identical, although you can use different pairs for the master and slave sets if you want. We planned ahead and built both our Pentium 4 and Athlon with identical 80 GB Maxtor drives, just so we could construct this RAID.

Figure 4-56
Installing the ribbon cable to the boot drive

We attach another 80-conductor ribbon cable to the IDE 2 connector. The 1200A shipped with two identical cables, which we would normally use, but we had an identical cable of a different color available, which makes the picture a little clearer. Our RAID 1 array increases performance when the array is read, as different stripes of data can be read from both drives simultaneously; but the performance during writes is unaffected, because all the data must be written to both drives.

Figure 4-57
Attaching the second ribbon cable to the RAID controller

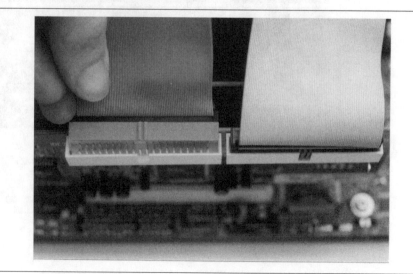

We install the black connector on the end of the IDE 1 ribbon cable to the second hard drive. Both drives must be jumpered as master, which is the default position for the white jumper as shipped from the factory. One of the features of the RAID BIOS software allows you to make a direct copy of the original drive on IDE 1 to the identical drive on IDE 2. Once the RAID is configured as bootable, we'll have a two-drive system with 100 percent data redundancy.

Figure 4-58
Attaching the ribbon cable to the second hard drive

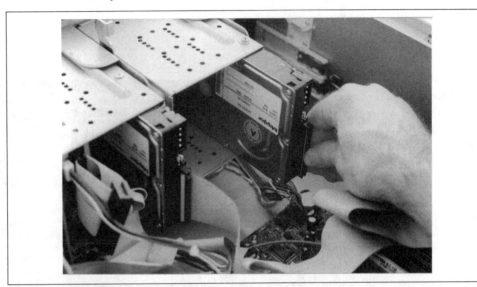

All that remains is to connect the power leads to our two hard drives, and the physical RAID assembly is complete. As soon as the system is booted, you'll need to install the RAID drivers in the operating system for viewing the event log and monitoring. Some of the RAID features are actually transparent to the operating system and can be configured either with the BIOS software or in the operating system.

Figure 4-59
Completed RAID hardware installation

The configuration screen shown below was actually shot after moving the RAID to our Athlon/Duron system where it will live. The RAID level is selected at the top of the screen and the drive status is shown at the bottom. The options hidden behind the RAID level selection box are

1. Create Array.

2. Delete Array.

3. Create/Delete Spare.

4. Select Boot Disk.

Figure 4-60
Adaptec
ATA RAID
configuration
screen

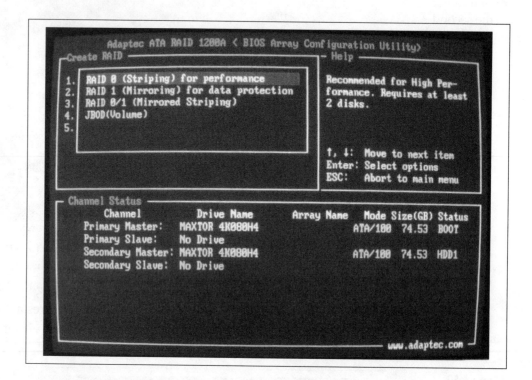

Option 2: A SCSI Subsystem

As discussed in the introductory chapters, a SCSI controller adds a whole new bus to your PC. Adaptec is far and away the dominant player in the SCSI controller market, and this Model 19160 supports Ultra SCSI with speeds up to 160 MB/s. The adapter is equipped with a high-speed 68-pin LVD/SE controller, and an older 50-pin Ultra SE connector. Don't mix high-speed and low-speed devices on the LVD controller, or the card will default to the lower speed.

Figure 4-61
Installing the
Adaptec 19160
SCSI controller

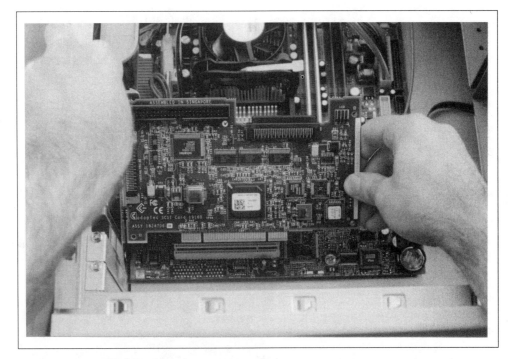

We'll skip showing the securing of the adapter with a screw (believe me, I took the picture) and move on to installing the SCSI drives. We chose to leave our IDE boot drive in place and install two SCSI drives in the second cage. The thin drive at the top of the cage is a brand-new 30 GB Maxtor Atlas 10K, a 10,000 RPM super high-performance drive. The thick drive at the bottom is an old-fashioned Fujitsu, which we included to illustrate the slow speed connector.

Figure 4-62
Installing the
drive cage with
two SCSI hard
drives

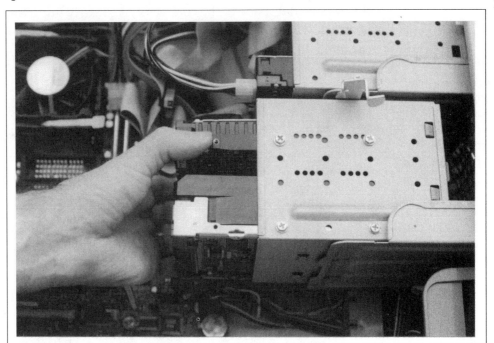

SCSI devices all have a set of SCSI ID jumpers, which is how the controller addresses them and prioritizes requests. The ID jumpers, four on new SCSI devices and three on the older ones, use binary selection. No jumper installed on an ID pair is a 0; a jumper is a 1. For older devices, ignore the leading 0 and use the top row. Also note that by default, SCSI controllers reserve ID 7 for themselves, which is assigned the highest priority. Bootable SCSI drives are traditionally given an ID of 0.

Jumpers	0000	0001	0010	0011	0100	0101	0110	0111
SCSI ID	0	1	2	3	4	5	6	7
Jumpers	1000	1001	1010	1011	1100	1101	1110	1111
SCSI ID	8	9	10	11	12	13	14	15

Figure 4-63
SCSI ID 5 selected on the Atlas 10K hard drive

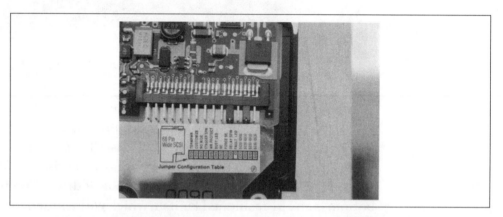

We begin by installing the 68 wire LVD cable to the SCSI adapter. Due to the trapezoidal shape of the connector, it's nearly impossible to get it on backward. However, you still want to take a good look and line it up correctly because the high density leads to thinner pins, which can get bent if you bash away blindly.

Figure 4-64
Connecting the LVD cable to the Ultra160 connector

The end connector on the SCSI cable is then attached to the Atlas 10K drive where it can only connect one way. Note the black terminator at the end of the cable that provides termination to the SCSI bus. When you purchase SCSI drives for this type of installation, don't pick a drive with a "hot swap" connector. These require special frame kits so the drive can be inserted or removed through the front of the case, and the drive sports a single connector to the frame kit, which is in turn wired to the standard SCSI and power cables.

Figure 4-65
Attaching the
LVD ribbon
cable to the
Atlas 10K drive

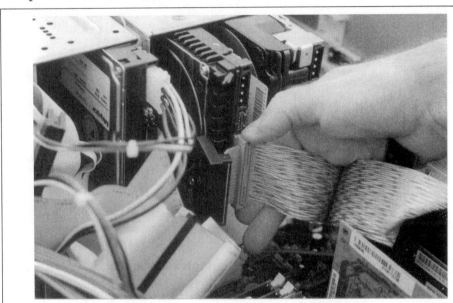

The old style 50-pin SCSI ribbon cable is attached to the SCSI controller. This controller actually provides two new physical buses to the system, each following its own termination rules, but they are combined as a single logical bus when it comes to device IDs. Termination on the controller is enabled by default. The LVD cable comes with a terminator at the end of the cable, but this 50-pin ribbon cable is unterminated.

Figure 4-66
Attaching the
50-pin ribbon
cable to the
Ultra SE connector

We attach the other end of the ribbon cable to the old Fujitsu drive whose connector is keyed just like IDE drives. Jumpers on the circuit board of the Fujitsu have been set with a SCSI ID and to enable termination. Some very old SCSI devices actually came equipped with resistor packs that were removed if no termination was required.

Figure 4-67
Connecting the 50-wire ribbon cable to the Fujitsu drive

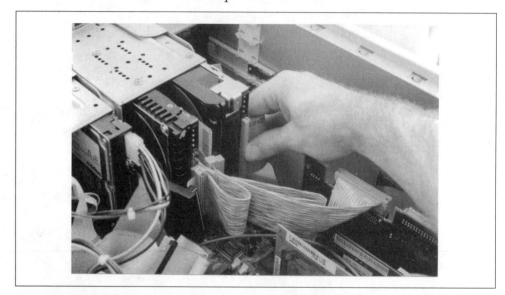

We skip passed the power connectors again to show the completed SCSI installation. The SCSI adapter ships with several instruction booklets and software for a variety of functions, such as managing SCSI tape drives and writing to SCSI CD recorders. If the ribbon cables hadn't been banded together, this case would be an incredible mess. PC manufacturers use special plastic clips for banding ribbon cables, which can often be found at stores like Radio Shack.

Figure 4-68
Completed SCSI installation

The BIOS on the SCSI adapter is accessed by pressing CTRL+A when the system is powered up. All the default values can be changed, but it's not advisable unless you have a conflict or compatibility issue with older SCSI devices. In the advanced settings, the communications parameters for each logical unit can be set independently.

Figure 4-69
SCSI configuration screen

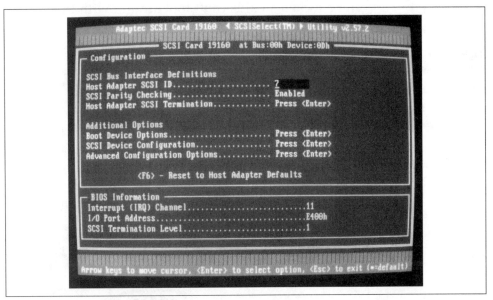

The status of all SCSI devices can also be viewed in the SCSI select utility. The most common error in assembling SCSI systems is setting ID jumpers improperly so that two devices share the same ID. This utility reports an error in that case and normally shows neither device as being present.

Figure 4-70
SCSI device status

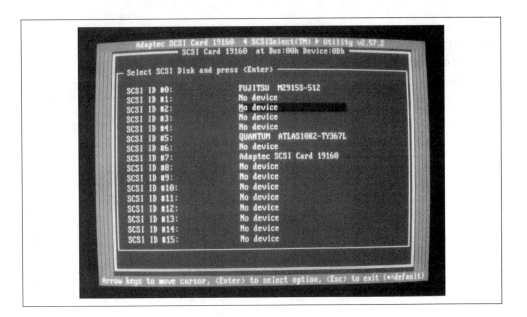

Step 8: Finishing Up

Let's take a final look at the front of our case with the door open. The three extra drive bays could be used for drives in frame kits, but in business and classrooms they are often used for multiple CD drives. Such drives can be accessed over the network, and in the classroom environment the front door can be locked so kids can't fool around with them.

Figure 4-71
Front view of
finished system

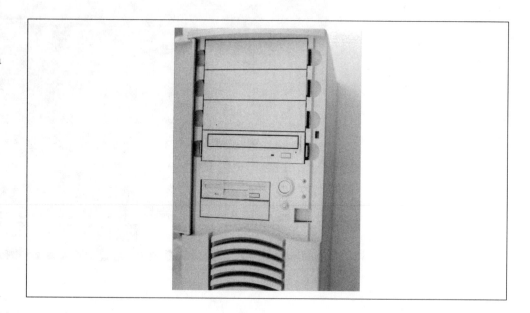

The case side or lid is installed the same way it came out and secured with two screws from the back. We decided to lock out the release handle once the lid was installed just for the sake of illustration. There are a finite variety of these circular keys, so they don't provide any great protection.

Figure 4-72
Locking out the
release handle

One of the last steps before plugging in the power supply is to check the voltage selector. We chose this system to show the switch in the wrong position for the U.S., 230 V, because it was actually sold to us this way! Turning on the PC with the wrong voltage selection will damage the power supply if you're lucky, and much more if you're not.

Figure 4-73
Checking the voltage selector

We're using a large paper clip here to slide the selector switch until the 115 V appears. To connect the power cord and make all the port connections, see step 10 of the Athlon/Duron build. Also note that the rocker switch to the left of the voltage selector is in the 0 down, or off, position. Once the system is plugged in, you can set the switch to 1 and leave it permanently on. The logic switch on the front of the PC is used to turn the PC on and off.

Figure 4-74
Setting the voltage to 115 V

The main screen of the Intel Setup Utility shows our 2 GHz Pentium 4, with a 400 MHz system bus, 256 KB of CPU cache, and two 128 MB PC800 RIMMs. For a detailed look at standard CMOS Setup options, see step 11 of the Athlon/Duron build.

Figure 4-75
Intel BIOS
Setup Utility

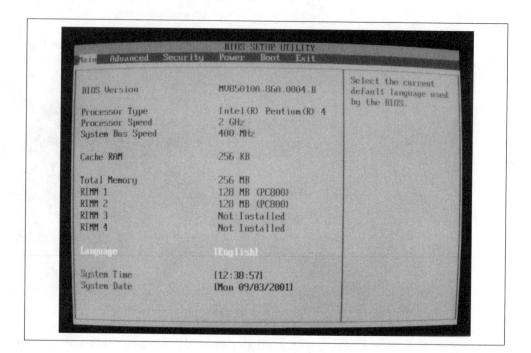

Chapter 5

Building an Athlon (Thunderbird) or Duron in a Midtower Case

Step 1: Preparing the Case

The first challenge facing the PC builder is often just how to open the case. There are no visible screws holding the sides of this case on, and the instructions are always packed away with the other accessories inside where you can't get at them! Hidden at the bottom of this front facade is a recessed latch. Stand the case on its back and lift the latch gently while keeping a hand over the facade to keep it from getting out of control. This is a habit that will come in handy when you need to open a finished system without tearing the faceplates off the floppy and CD-ROM.

Figure 5-1
Popping the latch

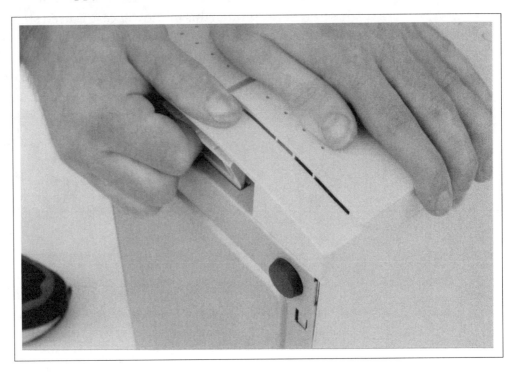

As the facade pivots away from front of the case on its open hinge, a circular fan grill comes into view. This case comes stock with an additional intake fan preinstalled, along with a 300W power supply. Don't assume that you have an additional fan because your case has a fan grill—most cases ship without one. Even though the fan is preinstalled, power will have to be connected at a later point.

Figure 5-2
Removing the
front facade

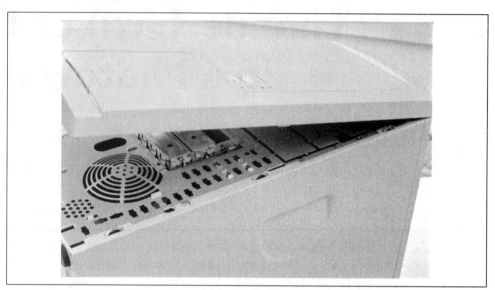

The sides of this case are secured by a series of interlocking metal tabs and a single screw. Even though this midtower case is used standing up, we refer to the side with the vent (rectangular area of perforations) as the top, because it will be directly over the motherboard. Because this case design uses rail mounted drives, we won't have to remove the other side of the case at all.

Figure 5-3
Removing a
case screw

Let's take a final look at the open case on its back. Note the cutouts down the left edge where the side panel locks into place. In addition to the power supply and chassis fan, the case contains a power cord and a box of parts, which includes drive rails, screws, a spare I/O core plate, and instructions.

Figure 5-4
An open case

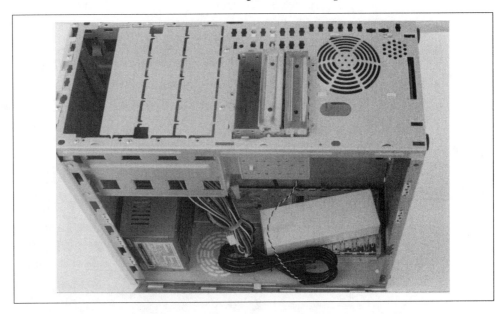

Before putting aside the facade, it's a good idea to remove the plastic blanks from the positions where you will install your drives. I actually forgot to do this once and slammed the facade onto a built system with a protruding floppy drive. Fortunately, that blank popped out without damaging the drive, but these are firmly held in place by plastic latching tabs.

Figure 5-5
Removing a floppy blank from the facade

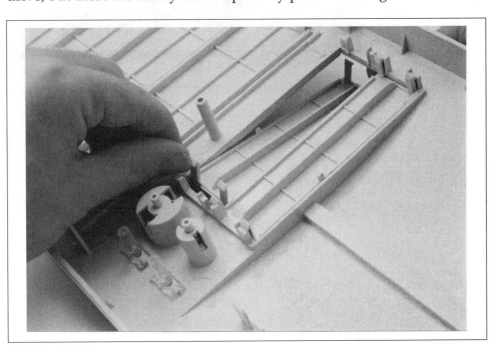

Step 2: Installing the CPU and Heatsink

We now move on to preparing the motherboard for installation. We chose a DFI (Diamond Flower International) Socket A board for this build. It can support the AMD Athlon with a 266MHz FSB (Front Side Bus) or the AMD Duron with a 200MHz FSB. The motherboard comes with a heatsink and fan preinstalled on one of the chipset chips. The two black slots at the bottom right of the motherboard are for the memory DIMMs and the I/O core is at the top right, directly above the white CPU socket. The board also sports six PCI slots for adapters and a 2X/4X AGP slot for the video card.

Figure 5-6
DFI 266MHz
Socket A
motherboard

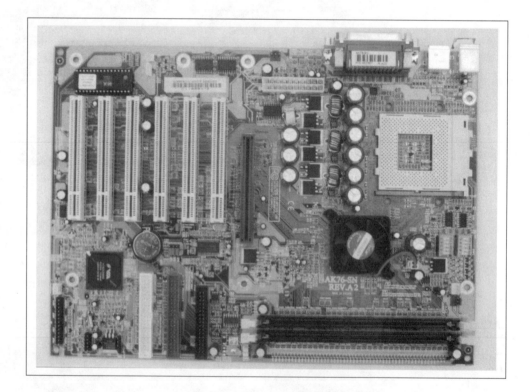

The first step to installing the CPU is lifting the locking lever on the socket. The lever is secured to the socket by a small ear on the side of the socket, which locks into a small indent in the lever. Pull the lever slightly away from the side before raising it to unlock the socket.

Figure 5-7
Lifting the
locking lever

The procedures for installing the Athlon and Duron CPUs in the socket are identical, as are the CPU packages. First, line up the two corners that have a corner pin missing matching corners on the socket. The CPU cannot be installed incorrectly without using a hammer or other serious coercion.

Figure 5-8
AMD CPU next
to Socket A

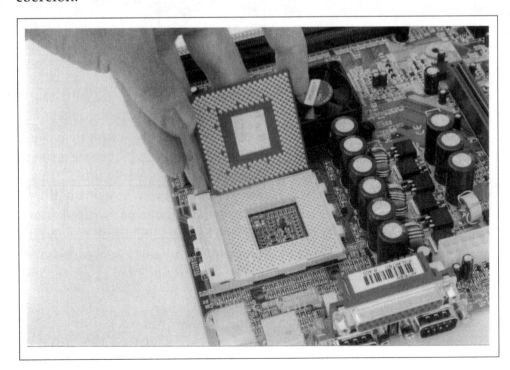

Lower the CPU directly onto the socket (don't lean it in from one side) until it sits perfectly flat. Visually confirm that all four corners of the CPU are flush with the socket before lowering the lever back into the locked position. Many first-time builders will be surprised by the amount of resistance the lever puts up. Just keep in mind that it is locking almost 400 individual pins in place by spring force. Also note that all four round pads on the corners of the CPU are intact, as they are crucial in positioning the heatsink on the CPU and protecting the silicon die.

Figure 5-9
Locking the CPU
into position

There are two variations of heatsinks in use with AMD CPUs, one of which uses a conductive thermal coating that is pre-applied to the heatsink and covered by a piece of tape, the other uses heat conductive grease. The purpose of these coatings is to fill microscopic gaps between the metal surface of the heatsink and the silicon chip in the center of the CPU package. Do not invent your own thermal coatings. If you buy a heatsink with a one-time coating and you make a mistake, go back to your parts supplier and get the approved grease. The main trick is to use very small amount and not drown the chip in grease. Apply a drop smaller than a pea to your (dry) finger tip and gently float it onto the protruding silicon chip without applying any pressure.

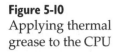

Figure 5-10
Applying thermal
grease to the CPU

Before placing the heatsink on the CPU, practice manipulating the spring to cause the passive side of the latching mechanism (the three metal clips; some heatsinks only use one) to protrude from the base of the heatsink. You can usually work the mechanism into a sweet spot, where clips will remain at their maximum extension without help. This is important because the heatsinks are bulky and the area around the CPU socket is usually so cramped that there will be no room for manipulating the clips when the heatsink is in place.

Figure 5-11
Manipulating the
heatsink latching
mechanism

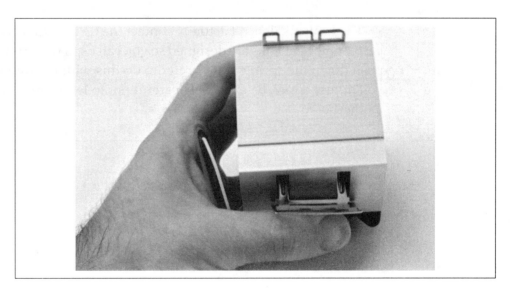

The indented edge of the heatsink mates with the base, or protruding area, of the socket. The Socket A heatsink cannot be latched and tilted down onto the CPU or damage to the chip will result. If you have room to manipulate the clips on your heatsink, you can place it directly over the CPU socket, and then slip the loop(s) over the protruding plastic stub(s). If there is no room to manipulate the clips, as in this case, place the heatsink flush over the socket and slide it a fraction of an inch toward the base to engage the loops.

Figure 5-12
Positioning the heatsink over the CPU and socket

The heatsink doesn't actually contact the CPU until it is latched over the base. Some heatsinks are designed so you can use a nut driver or other tool to push down the spring, but I prefer to do this with my thumb for control. If you do use a tool, be extremely careful not to let it slip off and damage the motherboard.

Figure 5-13
Locking the
heatsink to the
base of the socket

Immediately after installing the heatsink, connect the heatsink fan lead to the "fan1" connector on the motherboard. There is generally is an identical "fan2" connector available, the usual difference being that the motherboard is capable of monitoring and controlling the fan speed on "fan1" and not on "fan2." This is a useful feature for power saving modes.

Figure 5-14
Connecting the
heatsink fan to
the motherboard

The method of selecting the CPU voltage and clock multiplier varies from motherboard to motherboard, but most support automatic selection of both. The DFI motherboard ships with the selection switches for frequency and voltage set on Automatic, meaning the motherboard takes its settings from the CPU itself, but it pays to double-check the motherboard manual to ensure that the switches really are set as stated. The practice of setting the switches to manual override and choosing higher performance settings than the CPU is rated is known as *overclocking* and can result in damage to the CPU or operating problems.

Figure 5-15
Checking
switch settings

The final step in CPU installation is setting the FSB speed. On this motherboard this is accomplished using three jumpers set as a group to the 1–2 or 2–3 position. In this instance, the jumpers were not in the default (200MHz) position as stated in the manual, which shows that it pays to check.

Figure 5-16
Setting FSB
speed to 200MHz

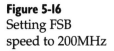

Step 3: Installing the Memory

In order to reach maximum performance with either the Athlon (266MHz FSB) or the Duron (200MHz FSB), we are building this system with a 256MB DDR (Double Data Rate) DIMM rated for 266MHz. Before inserting the DIMM in the memory socket, visually line up the single notch in the module with the positioning blank in the socket. Be careful not to touch the gold or silver contacts on the mating edge of the DIMM, even if you are securely grounded, because minute traces of oil from your skin can lead to a poor electrical contact.

Figure 5-17
Lining up the
DIMM with
the socket

Make sure that the white locking latches are all the way open (spread) before placing the DIMM in the socket and applying even pressure with your thumbs. As the DIMM settles into place, the white levers will raise themselves into the locked position. Never try to cheat the DIMM into place by digging in one corner first or raising one of the locking levers before it is seated.

Figure 5-18
Seating the DIMM with two thumbs

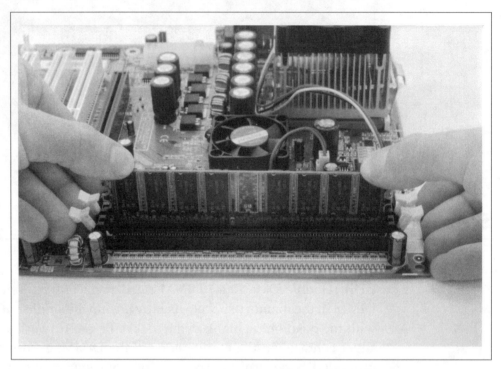

New motherboards allow you to use either memory socket when installing a single DIMM, but it's good practice to use the inboard socket, particularly when they are so close to the edge of the motherboard. Some PC builders prefer to install the memory after the motherboard is already secured in the case. Aside from the difficulties this presents to the photographer, it can actually result in flexing damage to the motherboard if the supports are too far from the memory sockets.

The motherboard is now prepared for installation in the case. Double-check that the CPU heatsink is properly secured and that the heatsink fan is connected to the "fan1" terminal. Also, locate the connector block for the front panel leads (power, reset, LEDs, speaker) and make sure the printing on the motherboard for these agrees exactly with the motherboard manual (they will be hard to read once the motherboard is installed). If there is a difference between the printing on the motherboard and the motherboard manual, it usually means that the motherboard revision is newer than the manual, and I go with the printing on the motherboard.

Figure 5-20
Motherboard
ready for
installation

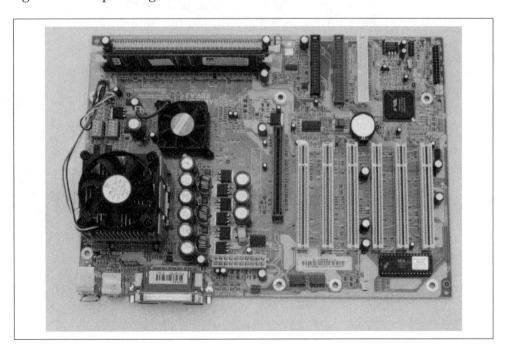

Step 4: Installing the Drives

This case is equipped with a removable 3-1/2" cage for the floppy drive and up to two internal hard drives. This cage is secured by a simple spring mechanism and a grooved track along its top. The cage is fairly flimsy, but it gains structural rigidity when the drives are screwed into place.

Figure 5-21
Removing the
3-1/2" drive cage

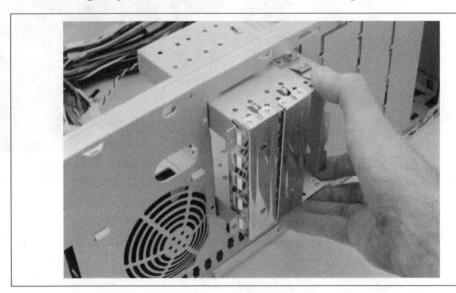

As we slide the floppy drive into the cage (label side up), you can clearly see the rails on the top of the cage, which slide into corresponding tracks in the case structure. These tracks carry the weight of the drives, as all tower cases are designed for operation in the upright orientation only. Also note that we install the drive in the closed end of the U-shaped cage first, usually the floppy. If you install the hard drive first, you might not be able to slide the floppy drive into place due to the deflection in the cage walls.

Figure 5-22
Sliding the floppy
drive into place

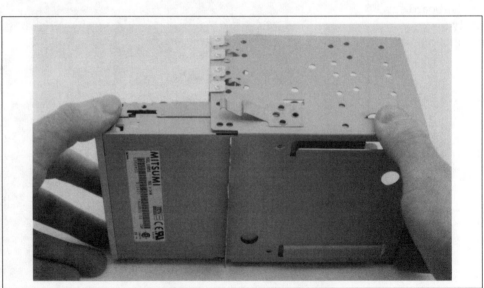

Secure the drive with four fine thread screws as soon as it is installed. Despite the large number of holes in the cage structure, you can normally determine the correct drive position as the one in which the maximum number of holes in the drive and the cage line up. In any case, the drive needs to be positioned to extend 1/2" or more beyond the front of the cage, so it will be flush with the front of the system when the facade is finally snapped into place.

Figure 5-23
Securing the floppy drive with four screws

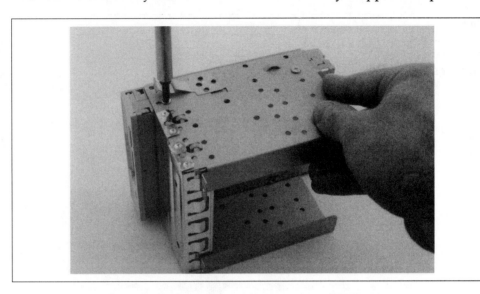

When installing a single hard drive in a cage, I always position it as far as possible from the floppy drive—to gain room for air flow—label side up, connectors toward the back. When installing two hard drives in a cage, make sure there is some room between them for air to circulate. If you are installing high-performance, multiple hard drives in a PC, it makes good sense to mount one or all of them in drive kits in the 5-1/4" bays to gain room for cooling air flow.

Figure 5-24
Sliding the Maxtor hard drive into place

Secure the hard drive with four course thread screws, two on each side of the cage. If your case came with flat-head screws, use these for securing the hard drive because screws with protruding heads may not clear the walls of the case when you install the cage. This 80GB Maxtor hard drive came in a retail pack that included a 5-1/4" frame kit, in case we want to mount it in an upper bay.

Figure 5-25
Securing the Maxtor hard drive with four screws

The cage should slide easily back into the case. Make sure the tracks on the top of the cage engage the case rails and that the cage doesn't droop when the springs lock into place. Normally, the cage can be further secured to the front of the case by three screws, but in this instance the holes for this purpose weren't tapped! Rather than trying to force screws through the metal, which can produce metal dust deadly to electronics, I judged that the cage was sufficiently secure on its rail and spring system, and the front facade adds a little more security when installed.

Figure 5-26
Sliding the cage into place

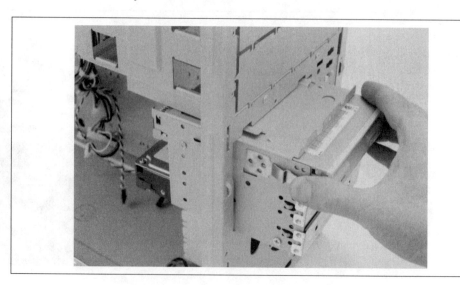

The 5-1/4" bays in this case are all designed to work with a rail system. These rails, which were popular in desktop cases 15 years ago, are making a strong comeback. The great advantage of rail-mounted drives is that after the initial rail attachment, they can be installed and removed from the case without fooling around with any screws. The rails are attached to the CDR with four screws, two for each rail. The spring end of the rail should end up about an inch from the faceplate of the drive so it can lock into place when the drive is still protruding enough to be flush with the facade.

Figure 5-27
Attaching the rails to the CD recorder

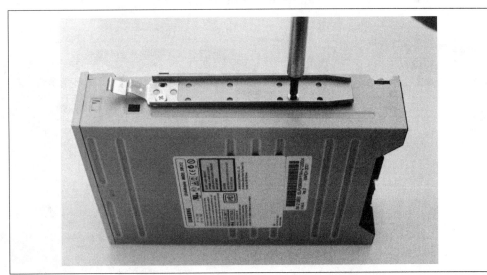

The other great advantage of having rail- and cage-mounted drives is that they can be installed without removing both sides of the case (see our Pentium III/Celeron build for contrast). Although I've never encountered a serious problem installing a rail-mounted drive, I have misjudged which screw holes to use more than once, resulting in a drive that fits only upside down until the rails are repositioned.

Figure 5-28
Installing the CD recorder

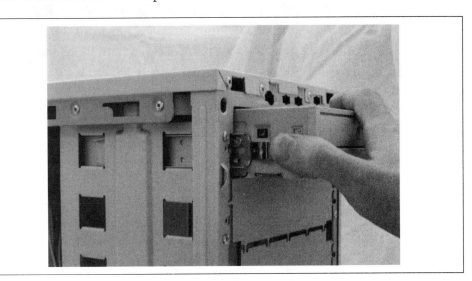

Step 5: Installing the Motherboard

The first step to installing the motherboard is a test fitting. Hold the motherboard by the edges with both hands and lower it into the case. Take careful note of where any existing standoffs (screw receptacles that hold the motherboard away from the case) are located, and how they line up with the existing holes in the motherboard. This is just a test fitting, so you're looking for the spots where there is obviously a standoff missing or one without a corresponding hole in the motherboard.

Figure 5-29
Test fitting the
motherboard

As with most new cases, this one shipped with standoffs installed in most of the standard ATX motherboard locations. However, there was an unsupported spot right by the I/O core where there are two standard possibilities for mounting, only one of which can be used. We installed a spring steel standoff with easy finger pressure in correct set of notches. Other common types of standoffs include brass hex-head screws with the head tapped to receive another screw and plastic snap-ins.

Figure 5-30
Installing a
missing standoff

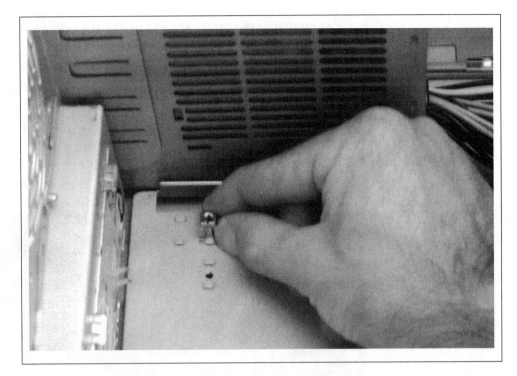

When you try to fit the motherboard over the existing standoffs but it doesn't come close enough to the back of the case, don't be surprised. The usual reason is that the I/O core includes more options, such as a second serial port in this case, than the default I/O shield. Note which protruding ports on the position the I/O core are lining up with metal blanks rather than openings. The offending port blank of the shield is removed by bending it back and forth against its breakaway tab.

Figure 5-31
Removing a
blank from the
I/O shield

Before you install the motherboard in its final home, count the number of standoffs installed in the case, and set aside that number of screws to secure the motherboard. If you end up with a leftover screw, stop; remove all the screws and take the motherboard back out. The #1 motherboard killer is probably the extra standoff that doesn't line up with a hole and grounds out the motherboard. Also, don't be surprised if it takes a little force to hold the motherboard in place as you put in the screws, starting with the corners. The reason is the grounding contacts on some I/O cores combine to apply a spring force trying to push the motherboard away from the back of the case.

Figure 5-32
Installing the final motherboard screw

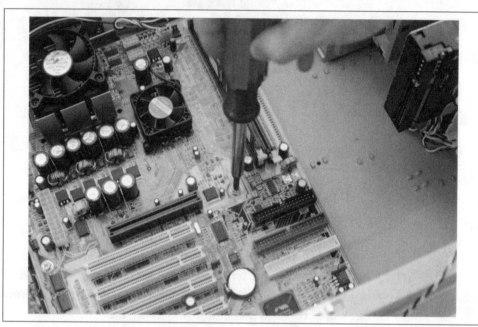

The ATX power supply connection to the motherboard for all CPU types except the Pentium 4 is a single 20-conductor connector. The connector only fits one way and is equipped with a plastic latch to hold it in place. If you need to remove the connector at a later time, just push in on the top of the latch (toward the wire bundle) while lifting.

Figure 5-33
Connecting the power supply to the motherboard

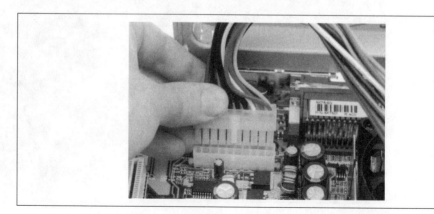

Even the most experienced PC builders often need to consult the motherboard manual for the proper positioning of switch and LED leads. These are usually located at the edge of the motherboard, near the front of the case. The speaker, reset, and power switch leads can be connected without worrying about polarity, but the LED leads for power and drive activity will only work one way. Here we are connecting the lead for the case speaker, which the system uses to report the outcome of the power on self test (POST).

Figure 5-34
Connecting the case speaker lead to the motherboard

Step 6: Connecting Power to the Drives

In this build, we will make all the power connections to the drives before moving onto the data connections. As you can tell by looking through the different builds in this book, it makes no difference in what order you make these connections as long as you make them correctly. We'll start with the CD recorder at the top of the case.

Figure 5-35
Connecting power to the CD recorder

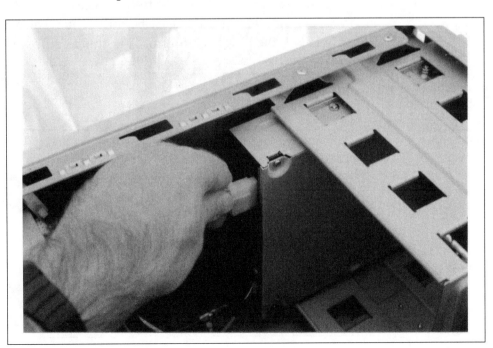

Normally, the only power connection that gives first-time builders any problems is the floppy drive. Unlike the larger power connectors used by hard drives and CD/DVD drives, floppy drives use a small format connector that can be forced on improperly. Normally, there is a flat tab under the four-pin power terminal on the drive that fits the rectangular depression in the power supply lead. Whereas all the connectors on the other drives are usually arranged in a line, on this floppy drive the power terminal is right next to the ribbon cable connector.

Figure 5-36
Connecting power to the floppy drive

The only trick with connecting the power to the hard drive is that it might take a reasonable amount of force to seat the connector. It doesn't have to go in all the way to the small ridge on the connector, often it can't, but it should go in far enough that it can't easily be pulled out. The small, white jumper directly below the power connector is in the default "master" position.

Figure 5-37
Connecting power to the hard drive

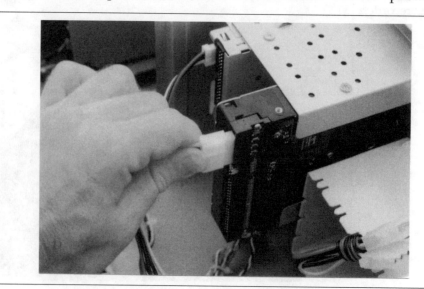

Our final power connection in this case is the additional case fan. This fan came preinstalled in the front of the case and uses a large format connector. The fan actually requires very little power and is equipped with a two-ended connector, so it can draw off the power it needs and you can still use the other end of the connector for powering a drive.

Figure 5-38
Connecting power to the case fan

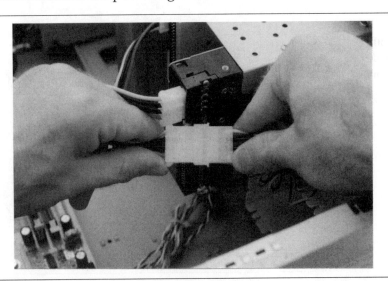

Step 7: Making Ribbon Cable Connections

The first ribbon cable connection we make is the CD recorder, using the older type 40-conductor IDE cable that shipped with the recorder. We connect the ribbon cable to the secondary IDE controller, making sure the red key wire is at the pin 1 end of the connector. Even though the motherboard connectors are keyed, the ribbon cables often aren't.

Figure 5-39
Connecting a ribbon cable to the secondary IDE controller

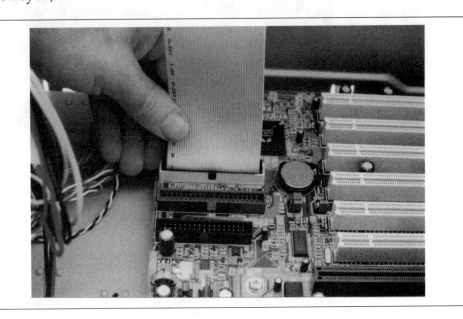

Here we show the ribbon cable attached to the CD recorder outside the system for clarity. The red key wire in the ribbon cable is matched to the pin 1 location on the drive connector. To the left of the ribbon cable on the back of the drive is the small white jumper in the "master" position, and to the left of it is the three-wire audio cable that is connected to the sound card for playing music CDs.

Figure 5-40
CD recorder connection

Next, we connect the blue end of the 80-conductor ribbon cable to the primary IDE connector on the motherboard. Many PC builders will always try to use the primary IDE channel to control both drives in a two-drive system, the hard drive as "master" and the CD or DVD as "slave". However, the newer CD/DVD drives sometimes go undetected by the system when installed as a "slave" device to the hard drive.

Figure 5-41
Connecting the 80-conductor ribbon cable to the primary IDE

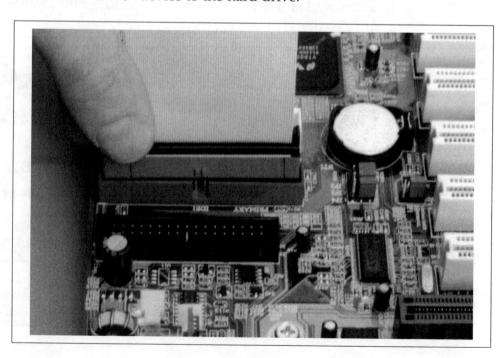

To achieve the 100 MB/s transfer rate a new hard drive like the Maxtor here is capable of, the "master" drive must be connected to the black connector on the ribbon cable. This is another reason to install the hard drive and CD or DVD drive on their own ribbon cables. Otherwise you either have to mount the hard drive in a 5-1/4" frame kit above the CD or DVD or really twist up the ribbon cable, possibly damaging it.

Figure 5-42
Connecting the black end of the ribbon cable to the hard drive

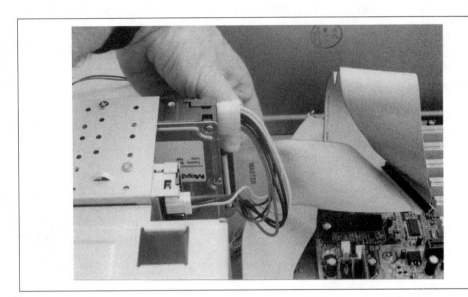

Finally, connect the floppy ribbon cable to the motherboard, making sure the red key wire is oriented to the pin 1 end of the connector. Some new motherboards ship with a very short ribbon cable for the floppy that only has two connectors, one for the motherboard and one for a single drive. I actually prefer these because it reduces cable congestion, and I don't recall the last time I used the second connector on a floppy cable that had one.

Figure 5-43
Connecting the floppy cable to the motherboard

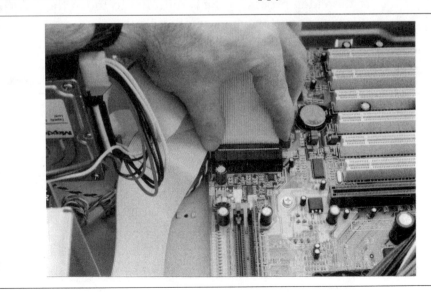

Possibly the most problematic connection in the whole PC is the floppy drive ribbon cable. Part of the problem is that at a wholesale price under $10, competition and innovation have vanished from floppy drive design and keeping the cost down takes priority. In any case, the connector on the vast majority of floppy drives is open and the cable can be mated incorrectly without a great deal of force. Make sure you locate the pin 1 end of the connector and match it with the red key wire in the ribbon cable.

Figure 5-44
Connecting the
floppy cable to
the drive

Step 8: Installing Adapters on the Motherboard

Our nVIDIA Sniper II video adapter is equipped with a 3D accelerator and 32MB of video RAM. The video adapter (actually called a "game card" by the manufacturer) is an AGP adapter capable of 2X or 4X operation and includes software for playing movies with a DVD drive. Note the passive heatsink on the video processor. Be careful not to touch the gold-plated fingers on the edge connector when you handle the card.

Figure 5-45
Installing the
AGP video
adapter

Install the hold-down screw in the video adapter immediately after seating it in the AGP slot. If you wait until you boot the system, the temptation to install the screw with the system hot might be overpowering, which could lead to disaster. Make sure the back end of the adapter doesn't pop partially out of the slot as the screw forces the front end down.

Figure 5-46
Securing the
video adapter
with a screw

The PCI sound card we chose supports up to 512 voices in synthesis, 3D sound effects, and compatibility with all the major standards. We take this opportunity to connect the CD sound cable that is directly attached to the back of the CD recorder. Without this connection, we would be unable to play music CDs on the system. Just make sure as you install the card that the cable doesn't get under the edge of the card and crushed into the slot.

Figure 5-47
Installing the
sound card

The adapter would be equally happy in any of the six PCI slots, but we needed to leave some healthy room between it and the heatsink on the video adapter. Like all new sound cards, it is jumperless. All configuration is handled by the software so you don't need to worry about removing it to play with interrupt and address jumpers. Most cases use the coarse thread screw to secure the adapters, but never try to force a screw in. The screws are generally of low quality and will break or flake under stress, and the last thing you want is tiny metal chips raining on the motherboard.

Figure 5-48
Securing the
sound card

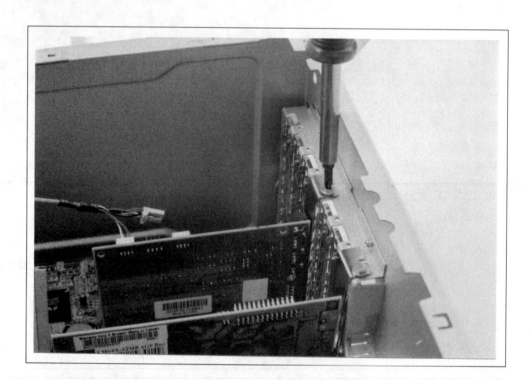

The final adapter in this system is the 56Kbs modem. Like all other modern adapters, the modem is jumperless, so it can be installed directly without worrying about interrupt or address settings. Unlike the integrated modem in our PIII/Celeron, this AOpen modem is a legitimate fax modem, which means you can send and receive faxes without buying special software or routing through the Internet.

Figure 5-49
Installing the
56Kbs fax/modem

Make sure you line up the telephone jacks on the modem card with the opening in the back of the case as you insert the screw. If you don't do this carefully, when you go to install the cord, it clicks right in; but if you need to get it out again, you find that the tab is stuck behind the case structure. That, coupled with the fact that accidentally installing the phone cord in the wrong jack under a dark desk is so common that I can't count the times I've done it wrong, makes it worthwhile to get it right the first time.

Figure 5-50
Securing the
modem with
a screw

Step 9: Closing the Case

Before you close the case, lift it off the table with both hands and gently tilt it back and forth through all the possible angles while listening for any loose screws rolling around. If you hear a screw starting to roll but then the sound goes away, that doesn't mean you're in good shape. Rather, you'll have to find the screw, by visual inspection if possible, but in the worst case take out the motherboard again to track down the one that got away. The side cover is then latched into place.

Figure 5-51
Restoring
the cover

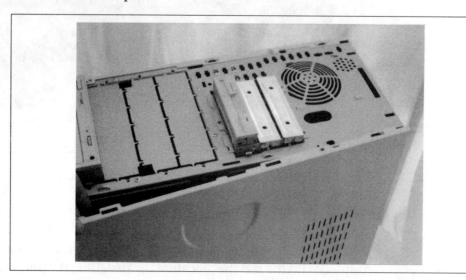

Many side covers actually require that you get locking tabs on two sides mated simultaneously, a sort of trick motion you acquire with practice. If you have trouble, just be patient and don't force it, eventually the cover will drop right in place for you. Make sure the cover is absolutely flush with the sides of the case before securing it with the single screw.

Figure 5-52
Securing the
cover with
a screw

Front facades vary greatly from case to case. Some are snapped into place with collapsible springs loosely resembling egg beaters at every corner. Others, when the case sides are secured from the back, are actually screwed into place. This facade has a simple open hinge at the top that aligns the facade correctly as it is lowered over the drives.

Figure 5-53
Hinging the
facade into place

Whether your facade is hinged into place or lowered directly onto the front of the case, go slowly to make sure that the plastic face plates on the drives line up properly with the openings in the facade. As you can imagine, if you need to remove the facade at a later date you must be very gentle to avoid pulling the faceplates off the drives, which can damage them.

Figure 5-54
Snapping down
the facade

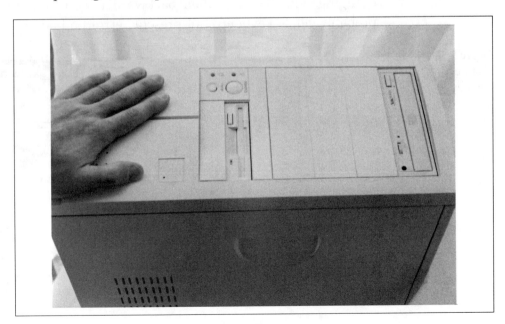

Step 10: Connecting the Peripherals

The time to double-check that the voltage switch on the back of your power supply is set correctly for your power grid is before you insert the power cord. The proper voltage for your country (115V for the U.S.) should be showing on the switch. The power cord can't be inserted improperly, but it can be inserted too shallowly, so make sure it pushes in a good 1/2 inch. The override rocker switch, if so equipped, should be switched on by pushing in the side labeled "1".

Figure 5-55
Connecting the power cord

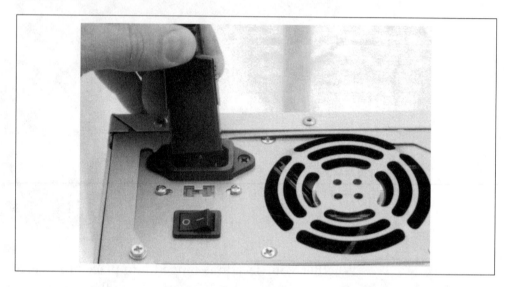

The keyboard and mouse ports are right next to each other and both use PS/2 style connectors. Almost all ports and connectors are color coded, purple for the keyboard and green for the mouse, to help you keep from interchanging them. If you get them backward, it won't hurt anything, but you'll probably get a "keyboard not present" error on boot.

Figure 5-56
Connecting the keyboard and mouse

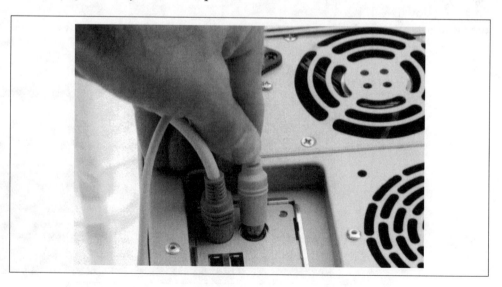

The monitor connector is a high density, 15-pin D-shell arranged in three rows, although a few pins are normally left out. Be careful that you get the orientation correct (it will only go on one way) and that you don't try to force it. The pins aren't very strong and if you bend one by hurrying, it might break when you try to straighten it. I once spent three hours soldering up a new end on a monitor cable; the density of the pins requires a thin soldering iron and steadier hands than mine.

Figure 5-57
Connecting
the monitor

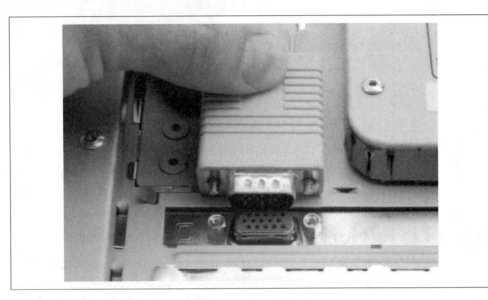

The external speakers are connected to the sound card through the speaker jack. The connection is a normal mini-stereo jack that has three contact areas: left channel, right channel, and ground. The line jack is for unamplified audio and the mic jack allows you to record your own voice or do speech recognition. The 15-pin port on the sound card is for attaching a joystick.

Figure 5-58
Connecting
the speakers

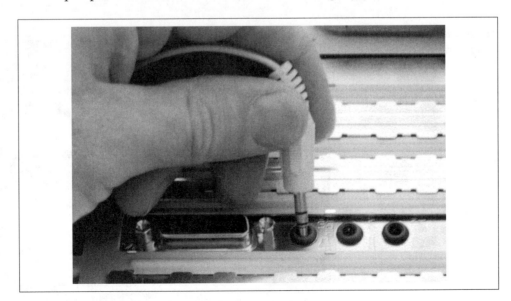

The modem port labeled "line" is connected to the phone jack on your wall using the phone cable that comes with the modem. If you have a telephone connected to the wall jack, you can reconnect it to the phone port on the modem. The telephone will work whether the computer is on or off, providing the line isn't in use by the modem or another extension.

Figure 5-59
Connecting
the modem

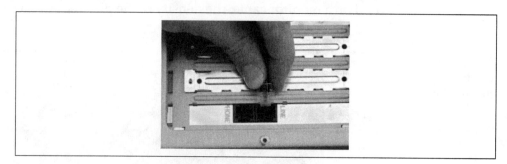

The PC, monitor, and any other peripherals attached to the PC should be plugged in to a common power strip with a surge protector. The common ground will eliminate the possibility of ground current loops.

Step 11: Exploring CMOS Setup

When you enter CMOS Setup, usually pressing the DEL or F1 key right after the PC is powered up, you are presented with the Main Setup screen, a menu of major setup functions. The items with an arrow to the left will present their own submenu; the items without arrows fulfill a single function. One of the most important single function items is Load Fail-Safe Defaults. This option disables memory caching, high-speed drive access, and all performance enhancing features for troubleshooting. Load Optimized Defaults restores all these settings to where you really want them.

Figure 5-60
Main Setup screen

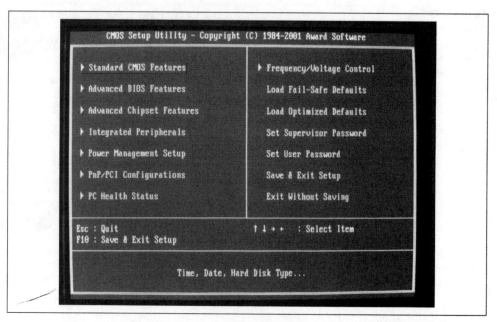

Standard CMOS Features, once the most frequented page in Setup, has lost most of its reason for existence to automatic drive detection. About the only occasion for which you might need to change settings here is if you are using a hard drive from an older system. If that's the case, before removing the drive from your old clunker, enter Setup there and write down the drive parameters and addressing mode (CHS, LBA, Large). When it's installed in your new system, select that hard drive on this screen and make sure the parameters match in the submenu (note the arrow to the left of the IDE items). If not, change from Auto to Manual and enter them by hand.

Figure 5-61
Standard
CMOS Setup

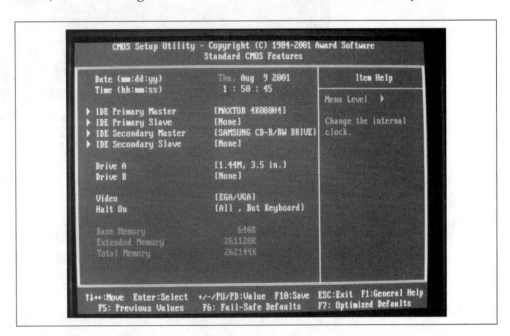

Although there are many user-configurable settings in Advanced BIOS Features, most should be left at the default settings unless you are trouble-shooting. (For example, you never want to use a PC with the internal or external CPU cache turned off.) However, you can arrange the order in which the system will try boot devices here, particularly if you have trouble installing your operating system on a new system. It's also the place to change the boot-up status of the NUM LOCK key, which controls the numeric keypad on the far right of the keyboard and drives some of us nuts!

Figure 5-62
Advanced BIOS
features

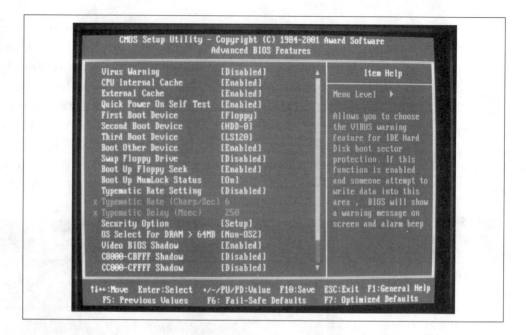

Advanced Chipset features defines how the motherboard chipset manages the onboard resources. Unless you are troubleshooting, you definitely want the system and video BIOS set "cacheable" so they can run at the speed of system RAM and not the Flash memory they are stored in. Also, if you are using Error Code Correction (ECC) memory DIMMs, you can tell the chipset how to handle error conditions; whether to stop dead and report or fix the error and continue.

Figure 5-63
Advanced Chipset
features

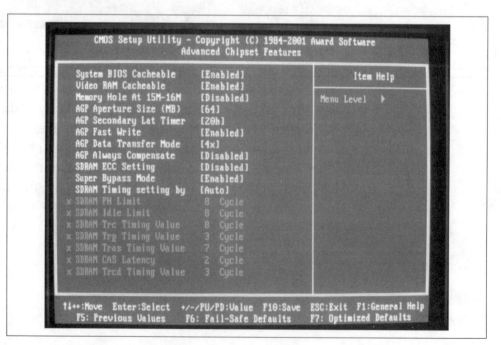

Integrated Peripherals includes all the onboard peripheral controllers, such as the IDE controllers, USB ports, I/O ports and printer port. Generally, the default Auto selection is fine, but in troubleshooting, you may want to cut back the speed of the IDE bus (or temporarily disable DMA). You can even disable the IDE controllers entirely, replacing them with a PCI IDE controller. Note the vertical bar to the right of the menu area that indicates the whole screen isn't shown. You'll have to scroll down to get to the second serial port or the printer port.

Figure 5-64
Integrated
Peripherals

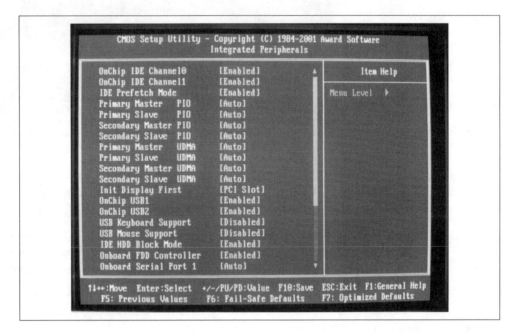

Power Management encompasses not only power conservation settings but all power up and down functions. Here you can instruct the PC to come out of standby (a low power sleep mode) on modem, network, or other PCI adapter activity. You can also control how the power switch on the front panel functions, with a four-second delay or with immediate results. An important feature for servers is whether you want the PC to automatically power back up after a power outage shuts it down.

Figure 5-65
Power
Management

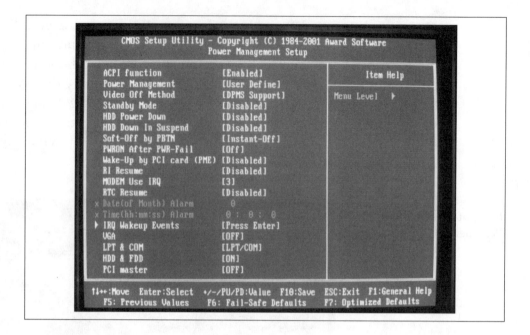

PnP/PCI Configuration is another screen that you can leave alone if everything works, but which is invaluable for troubleshooting or getting older legacy adapters to work. You'll usually want to select PNP OS Installed (i.e., you are using a Plug and Play operating system such as Windows). If you can't get the operating system to recognize or allocate resources to an older adapter, you can allocate the resources manually here, IRQ and DMA, on a slot-by-slot basis. Also, if you try adding a new adapter to your PC and can never boot up afterward, you can try enabling Reset Configuration Data.

Figure 5-66
PnP/PCI
Configuration

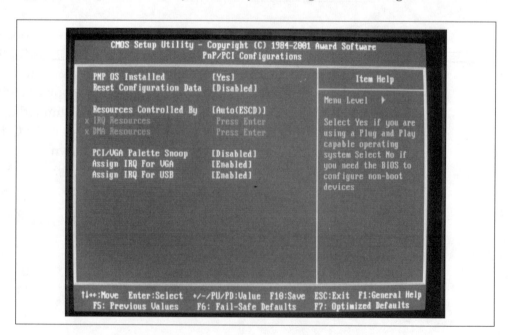

PC Health Status is the PC equivalent of the monitoring screens around a hospital bed in ICU, which hopefully you've only seen on TV. Not only is it helpful for troubleshooting overheating conditions and power supply problems, but it allows you to set a ceiling temperature at which the PC will shut itself down to prevent damage. The CD that ships with the motherboard usually contains a program that will display all this information from within your operating system.

Figure 5-67
PC Health Status

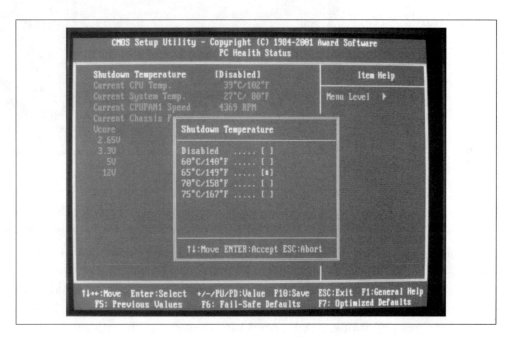

Frequency/Voltage Control is strictly for overclockers—techs who choose to exceed the manufacturer recommended settings for their CPUs and memory. The main dangers are overheating and instability, so the frequency control allows you to raise the basic clock speed in 1MHz increments while monitoring performance. Another side effect of overclocking can be shortened component life, though this isn't much of a concern to someone who wants the performance now. Frankly, I haven't fooled around with overclocking for more than 10 years because all the stuff seems awfully fast to me these days.

Figure 5-68
Frequency/
Voltage Control

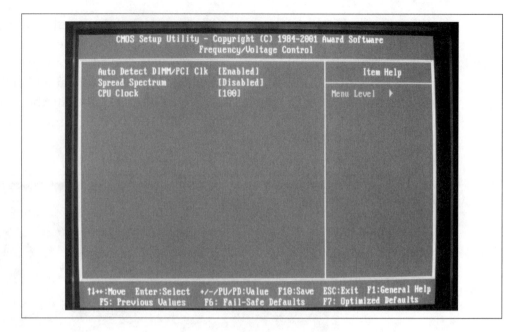

None of the changes in CMOS Setup take effect unless you choose Save | Exit, which you can reach directly from most Setup screens by pressing the F10 key. The two options on the Main Setup screen that we didn't mention are the Supervisor Password and User Password. The main reason most people might want to set a Supervisor Password is to prevent their kids from accidentally putting in a password and forgetting what it is, effectively cutting off access to the PC or Setup (password prompting is controlled by Security Options in Advanced BIOS Settings). The sole cure for a lost password is to open the PC and place the "discharge battery" or "forget password" jumper on the motherboard.

Figure 5-69
Save settings
and exit

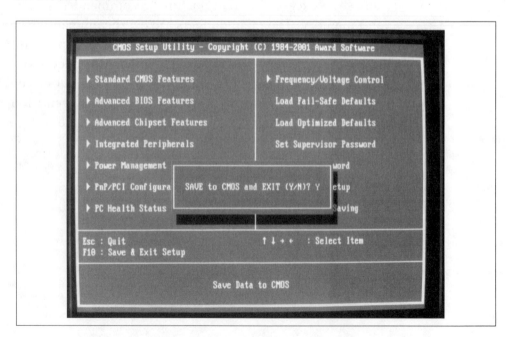

Chapter 6

Building a Pentium III or Celeron in a Minitower Case

Step 1: Preparing the Case

This minitower case is an innovative design that offers both benefits and drawbacks. Part of the reason for choosing this case was variety, since we illustrated two midtower builds with the Pentium 4 and Athlon/Duron systems. The unique feature of this case is the power supply, which is latched into position and secured with one thumb screw. The case is somewhat cramped to work in, but it results in a compact system and is a good match for the highly integrated motherboard we chose.

Figure 6-1
New minitower
from the rear

Like most new designs, the case cover consists of three separate lids, rather than one piece. Once the system is assembled, the motherboard can be accessed by removing two screws on the up side rather than a whole cover. Although the minitower is obviously designed to stand up, we work on it laid on one side, in the position where the I/O core is at the bottom. Begin by removing the side lids, each of which is held by two screws in the back of the case.

Figure 6-2
Removing a screw
from the lid

The lid is slid straight back about 1/2" to disengage the metal tongues from the edges of the case, then lifted straight up. When building a minitower without a hinged power supply, the motherboard pan is usually removed and the motherboard mounted outside the case. However, because the power supply can be removed entirely and there is no blocking support, the motherboard can be installed directly into the system.

Figure 6-3
Case with the
top lid off

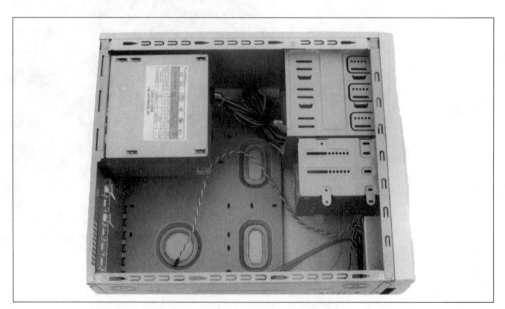

Remove the box or bag with the spare parts and accessories from the case, and install the plastic or rubber feet on the case bottom, which will keep the case from scratching the table or floor. These feet are often preinstalled on newer cases.

Step 2: Mounting Memory on the Motherboard

The motherboard is removed from a static-proof bag and laid on a hard, flat surface on top of the thin, nonconductive foam with which it came. The three long, black sockets with the white locking levers to the lower right of each end are the DIMM sockets. The motherboard chosen was one of the most highly integrated motherboards available, including sound, AGP video, a 56Kb/s modem, a 10/100BaseT network adapter, and the option to install either Slot 1 or Socket 370 Intel processors.

Figure 6-4
Motherboard fresh
out of the box

A single 64 MB DIMM is installed by aligning the notch in the bottom edge of the DIMM with the key in the DIMM socket. With some motherboard designs, the first (or only) DIMM installed in the system must be placed in first bank, labeled "DIMM 1" on this motherboard. The white levers to either side of the socket must be spread before you attempt to insert the DIMM.

Figure 6-5
64 MB DIMM
over the socket

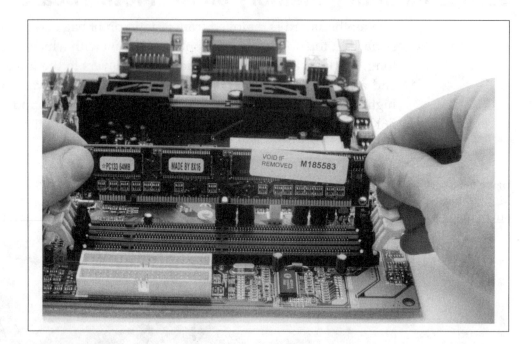

Push evenly on the DIMM with a thumb on each end. The locking levers should slowly draw in until the DIMM is fully seated. Sometimes, a little wiggling and some heavy pressure are needed, but you should never dig one end of the DIMM into the socket first and try to force down the other end after it.

Figure 6-6
Seating DIMM
with even pressure

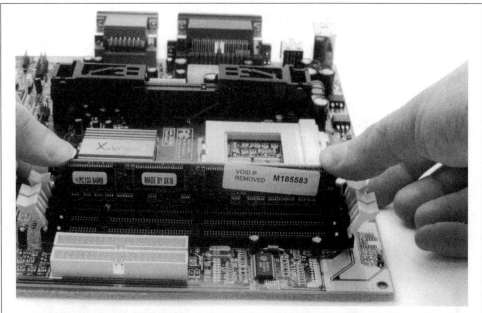

The DIMM is now seated perfectly in the socket. Note that the white locking levers are fully engaged. When the PC is powered on for the first time and you enter CMOS Setup to set the CPU speed, you should also make sure that PC-133 memory is set to a speed of 6 nS and PC-100 DIMM is set to 8 nS. Otherwise, they will run at a slower default. Because only one memory speed setting is possible for the system, avoid mixing modules of different speeds in a system.

Figure 6-7
DIMM properly
installed on
motherboard

Step 3a: Pentium III Option

The first step with such a flexible motherboard is to select the CPU package being installed. This is done with a jumper right next to the sockets, as detailed in the manual that comes with the motherboard. For variety, we will install a Pentium III in Slot 1, and as a variant path, a Celeron in Socket 370. New Pentium IIIs are more likely to be Socket 370 than Slot 1 devices, but we try to cover all the bases in this book.

Figure 6-8
Setting the jumper to Slot 1

Next, raise the folded Slot 1 supports that will receive the Pentium III. On many Slot 1 motherboards, the supports are supplied separately and must be snapped into or screwed to the motherboard. Some older Slot 1 Celerons required a CPU retention bracket that bridged the supports and held the CPU in place.

Figure 6-9
Raising the
Slot 1 supports

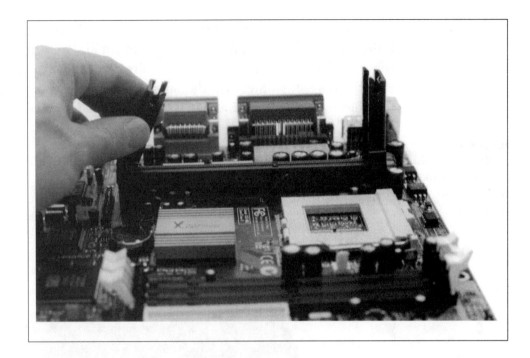

This Pentium III processor is a Single Edge Contact Cartridge 2 (SECC2) for Slot 1 motherboards. Both the Pentium III and the motherboard are capable of a 100 MHz front side bus, and newer versions of the Pentium III are capable of 133 MHz bus operation.

Figure 6-10
Pentium III

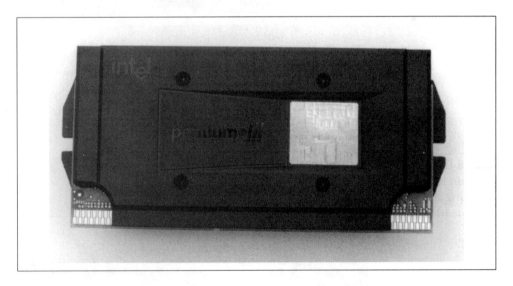

We have actually disassembled the Pentium III fan and heatsink to illustrate that the fan is a replaceable unit. Almost all Pentium III SECC processors are sold with the heatsink and fan already installed, primarily to reduce the chances a customer will damage the cartridge mounting these snap-together units or attempt to use it without an active cooling device.

Figure 6-11
Pentium III from back—heatsink with the fan removed

The fan assembly snaps over the four plastic posts projecting from the heatsink. When plugged into the proper fan power point on the motherboard, the fan can be controlled by the power management logic in the BIOS. The power supply in this minitower also has an intake grill in its bottom to draw hot air away from the processor.

Figure 6-12
Pentium III—snapping the fan onto the heatsink

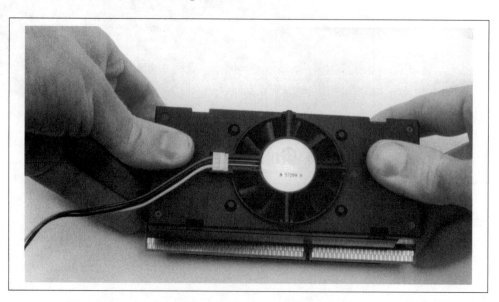

As with the previously installed DIMM module, the edge of the connector on the Pentium III has a notch to one side that matches a key in the socket. Double-check that you are lowering the Pentium III in the right orientation because it can take a good deal of pressure to properly mate a Slot 1 connector.

Figure 6-13
Lowering
Pentium III
into Slot 1

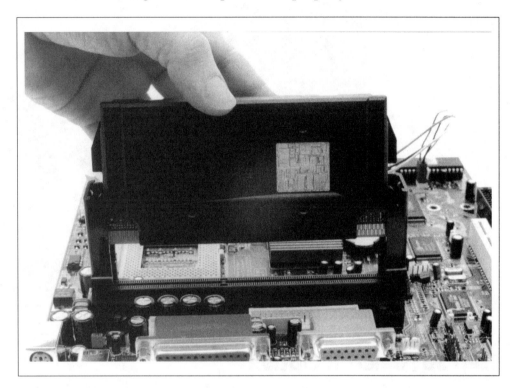

If your Pentium III package is equipped with compressible tabs on either end, hold these in while lowering the processor into the slot. Otherwise, use your thumb to push on either end of the Pentium III, just like with the DIMM module, until you feel the Pentium III snap into place. The most common reason a new Slot 1 system fails to boot is a processor that isn't seated all the way.

Figure 6-14
Pentium III
properly seated

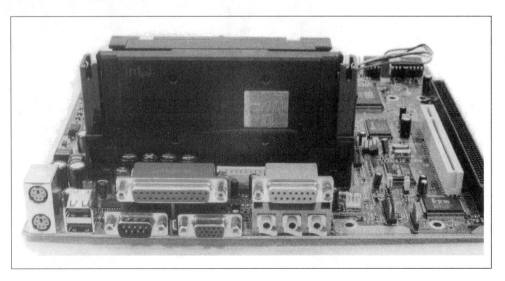

Check the motherboard manual to see which of the several fan connection points on the motherboard is for the heatsink fan. This is commonly the "fan1" connector, but it is found in a different place on every motherboard.

Figure 6-15
Connecting the heatsink fan to the motherboard

Step 3b: Celeron Option

Using the same motherboard, we will install a Socket 370 Celeron processor. As with the Pentium III, the first step is to select the CPU mounting that will be used. In this case, move the jumper to the Socket 370 position.

Figure 6-16
Setting the jumper for Socket 370

The Celeron package for Socket 370 is very similar in appearance to the old Socket 7 design, but the two are mutually incompatible. The PPGA (Plastic Pin Grid Array) packages for Socket 370 are lacking the corner pin on two corners, as opposed to one corner for Socket 7 chips.

Figure 6-17
Celeron processor for Socket 370

The Celeron cannot be installed in a Socket 370 incorrectly because of the two keyed corners. The first step to installing the Celeron is to lift the locking lever at the side of the socket all the way up to the vertical position. Then, match up the corners of the chip to the socket and lower it directly into place.

Figure 6-18
Checking proper Celeron alignment with the locking lever up

The Celeron must seat perfectly flat in the socket. If it doesn't seem to want to sit all the way down, double-check that the locking lever is all the way up and that it didn't start in cocked to one side. Once the Celeron is seated properly, the lever action may be fairly stiff as you lock it in place. The lever must return all the way to the tuck position alongside the socket.

Figure 6-19
Lowering the locking lever

The heatsink and fan for Socket 370 processors are locked over the Celeron to the socket, not to the Celeron itself. The same heatsink and fan can be used for any Socket 370 processor, which requires less cooling than Athlon or Pentium 4 CPUs.

Figure 6-20
Heatsink with a fan

The first step to install the heatsink is to slide the steel spring all the way to one side of the heatsink; then hook that side over the back of the plastic ear on the Socket 370 base.

Figure 6-21
Hooking the spring onto the back of the base

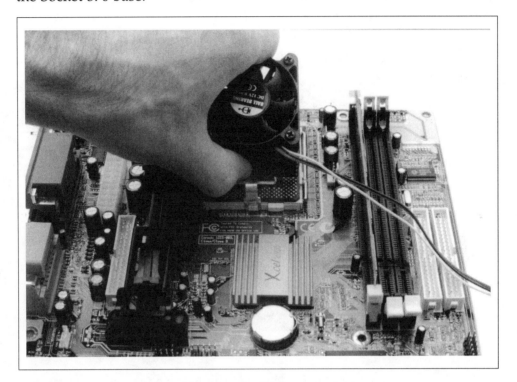

The next step is to slide the heatsink back down the spring so that it aligns with the edge of the Celeron. Then lower the heatsink assembly over the Celeron, keeping the heatsink squarely over the chip.

Figure 6-22
Lowering the heatsink over the Celeron

When the heatsink is flat over the socket and squarely over the chip, push the spring down over the plastic ear on the front of the socket. It's best to do this with your thumb while firmly holding the heatsink assembly in place with your hand.

Figure 6-23
Locking the heatsink in place

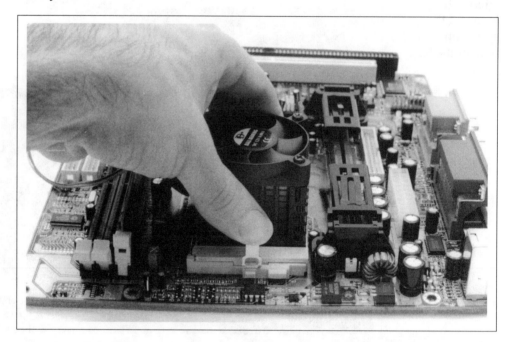

After the heatsink is installed, the fan lead is connected to the fan1 power point. While you have the motherboard manual open to find the fan1 connector, it's a good time to familiarize yourself with the other connectors on the motherboard, because once it is installed in the case, you might find your view of these partially obstructed by other components.

Figure 6-24
Connecting power to fan1

Step 4: Mounting the Motherboard

The instructions for mounting the motherboard and assembling the rest of the system are identical with either the Pentium III or the Celeron in place. The first step, with this particular case design, is to remove the power supply to gain access to the motherboard pan. The power supply is held in by a single thumb screw with a large plastic head, which is removed by hand.

Figure 6-25
Removing the power supply thumb screw

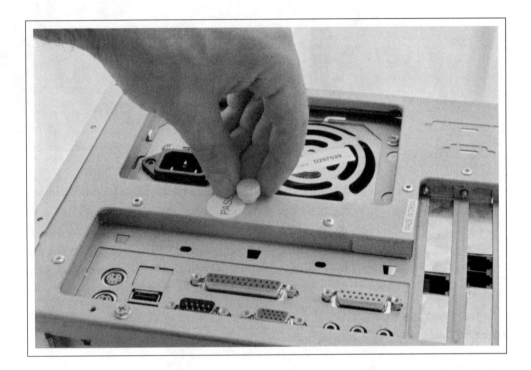

The power supply now hinges up on the back of the case and is lifted out. The geometry of this case almost necessitates this easy-out feature because the power supply, when installed, blocks access to the floppy cable, the CPU, and even to the power supply connection to the motherboard.

Figure 6-26
Removing the
power supply

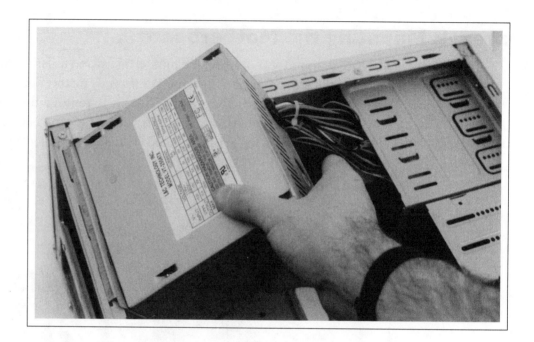

Now, place the motherboard in the case to check which punch-outs in the I/O core must be removed. Most motherboards ship with a foil I/O shield, which exactly matches the motherboard I/O core and fits in the standard ATX I/O opening (see the Pentium 4 tower system for a good illustration of this). This case comes with a standard shield installed, which has punch-outs that can be removed to match the motherboard I/O core.

Figure 6-27
Fitting the
motherboard
in the case to
check I/O core
alignment

After noting which punch-outs need to be removed, take the motherboard back out. While pushing with a Philips screwdriver or other reasonably blunt instrument to break the punch-outs free, use your other hand to hold the I/O shield from the back so it doesn't get bent out of shape. However, make sure your hand doesn't end up behind the punch-out, because even a blunt screwdriver will hurt if you stab it into your hand.

Figure 6-28
Punching out
a blank for the
sound connections

Now comes the tricky part. Place the motherboard back in the case and check that the I/O core matches up with the shield, so the motherboard is resting in its final position. Now look for the holes in the motherboard where you will be placing screw to secure it in the case. These holes are ringed by silvery solder. Try to remember where a couple holes near one side of the motherboard are, and then move it out of the way just enough to reveal the holes in the motherboard pan where the standoffs or screw receptacles will be installed.

After you get the standoffs on one side in, you'll have to remove the motherboard each time you line up new holes, because you don't want to drag it on the standoffs you've installed. The type of standoffs supplied with a case varies with the manufacturer, so look at the other systems in this book if the standoffs used here don't match yours.

Figure 6-29
Inserting a standoff in the motherboard pan (shown out of the case)

Spring steel standoffs can be inserted without any tools by gently squeezing them and putting them in place. Avoid using pliers or squeezing too hard, because the steel will stay bent and the standoff will rattle around until you get a screw in it. Use as many standoffs as will match holes in your motherboard and pan, six or seven in most cases, and count the number installed.

Figure 6-30
Standoffs installed in the motherboard pan

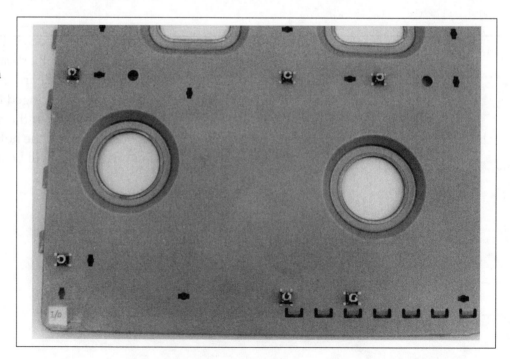

Finally, the motherboard is installed in the case for good. Double-check the I/O core to make sure all the ports on the motherboard are accessible. With a good light or flashlight, look through the mounting holes in the motherboard and make sure you can see the edge of all the standoffs you inserted before you start installing screws.

Figure 6-31
I/O core matched
through case back

Begin putting screws in the motherboard, but don't tighten them until all the screws are installed. If the number of screws used doesn't match the number of standoffs you put in, take it out again and remove the standoff that didn't line up.

Figure 6-32
Screwing in the
motherboard

Step 5: Making Connections and Reinstalling the Power Supply

Check for any other connection points that will be obstructed when the power supply is installed. We find that with this motherboard, the floppy drive connector will end up under the power supply. On checking the motherboard manual for the proper cable orientation, we also find that the pin 1 orientation of the floppy connector is the reverse of the IDE connectors. This is rare for motherboards, which generally keep all connections oriented the same way; and it goes to show that you should always check the manual.

Figure 6-33
Attaching the floppy cable with the red wire keyed to pin 1

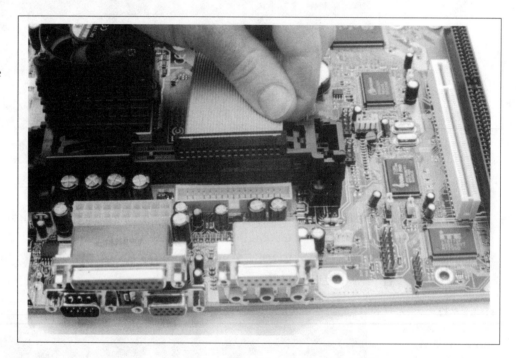

The ATX power supply connector consists of 20 wires in a single snap-on unit and is keyed to fit only one way. Because the connection point on the motherboard ends up under the power supply itself, it's necessary to make this connection before putting the power supply back in. We show these connections with the motherboard out of the case for clarity, but you'll make them with the motherboard installed.

Figure 6-34
ATX power supply
connection

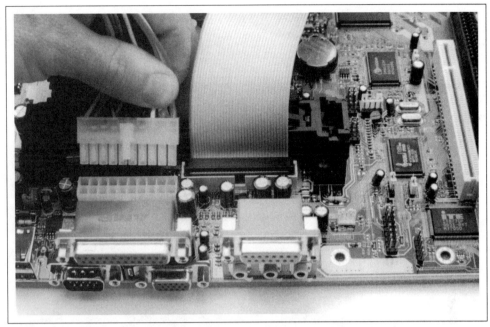

Before reinstalling the power supply, check that the 115/230 V switch located on the back of the supply is on the correct voltage for your country. This is 115 V in the U.S., and 230V in most other countries, but if you aren't sure, find out.

Figure 6-35
Check the voltage
switch on the
power supply

Return the power supply to the case, hinging it over the top edge and then lowering it into position. Put the thumb screw back in immediately afterward so it doesn't get forgotten.

Figure 6-36
Reinstalling the power supply

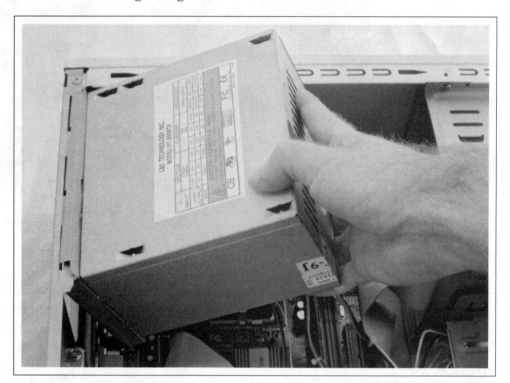

Step 6: Installing the Adapter Risers

Almost all PCs will be built with at least one add-on adapter, but this motherboard is an exception. All the basic adapter functions are onboard: AGP video, 56Kb/s modem, 10/100BaseT network adapter, and full sound capability. However, the standard I/O core doesn't provide enough room to accommodate the network and modem ports, so the motherboard manufacturer provides adapter risers, which are little more than a slot plate with a port, although a small circuit card is included.

Figure 6-37
Adapter risers

The network riser is then connected to the motherboard by way of a small ribbon cable connection, which is kept short to reduce electrical noise. This requires that the riser be mounted in the slot nearest to the connection point. The ribbon cable is keyed with a red wire that must be connected to the pin 1 end of the connector.

Figure 6-38
Connecting the network riser cable

The adapter extender is screwed into place on the back rail. Always screw in any adapters or adapter risers immediately after you install them, making sure the port opening is fully exposed through the slot.

Figure 6-39
Screwing in the network riser

The modem riser on this motherboard is a more standard design than the network riser. Rather than wasting a cable, the modem riser is plugged directly onto the motherboard to a proprietary connection block that leaves no chance for backward connections.

Figure 6-40
Mounting the modem riser on the motherboard (shown outside case)

Seat the modem riser firmly, making sure it settles over both rows of pins; then install the screw. With all the integrated features on a motherboard like this, you don't need to buy or install any conventional adapters at all. However, if we did want to add more functionality to this system, there is only one shared ISA/PCI slot available.

Figure 6-41
Securing the modem riser

When the system is built with the Slot 1 Pentium III option, you can see what a tight fit the cabling is. Both the floppy cable and the power connector would have been impossible to install without first removing the power supply. Although the combination of a cramped case and a crowded motherboard is not ideal, you only have to put it together once. It does provide an excellent illustration of why you must always be thinking ahead to the next step, and why you should look over all the systems in this book to see what you might encounter.

Figure 6-42
Pentium III with the motherboard connections made

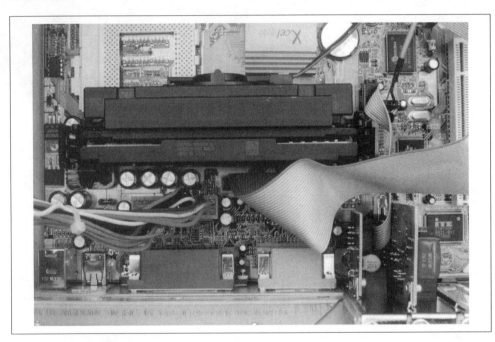

Step 7: Installing Drives

There are two connectors on a floppy drive and no jumpers you need to set. However, it is important to closely examine the drive before installing it in the case to note, which is the pin 1 end of the connector. Unlike hard drives and CD drives, floppy connectors are rarely built to accept keyed connectors, and when they are, they are occasionally keyed the wrong way.

Figure 6-43
The rear of the floppy drive

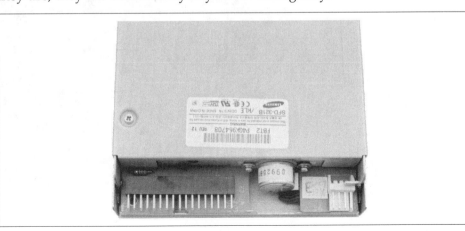

Remove the plastic blank from the front of the case where you will install the floppy drive by popping it out with your fingers from behind. Next slide the drive through in the upright position from the front of the case. Normally, we would preinstall the ribbon cable on the drive to avoid mistakes, but because the ribbon cable connection to the motherboard is so awkward in this system, we do it with the drive installed.

Figure 6-44
Sliding in the floppy drive

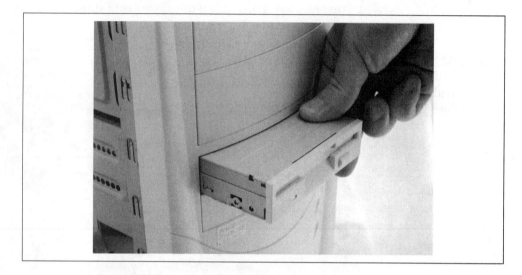

Secure the floppy drive with four screws as soon as you install it. It's much easier to install the cables with the drive solidly fixed in place so it doesn't yield when you push to make connections.

Figure 6-45
Securing the floppy drive

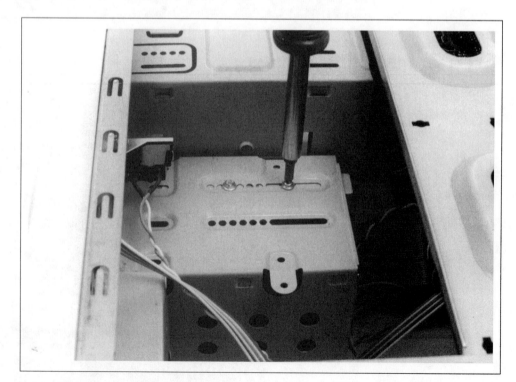

The ribbon cable goes on with the red key wire at the pin 1 end of the connector. Sometimes the drive connector is only labeled with a 33 or 34, which tells you pin 1 is on the opposite end. It's crucial to get the connector on without missing an entire row of pins or bending two out of the way at one end or the other. About 99 percent of the instances of floppy drives not working in new systems are because of the ribbon cable being pushed on wrong.

Figure 6-46
Installing the
ribbon cable

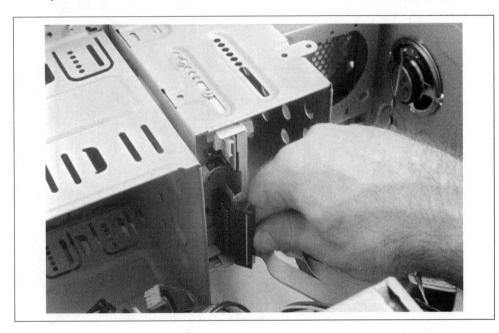

The power connector to the floppy drive is seated with the shallow cutout on the back of the small connector from the power supply over the plastic tab that extends over the four pins on the drive or down toward the circuit board if the plastic tab is absent.

Figure 6-47
Installing the
floppy drive
power lead

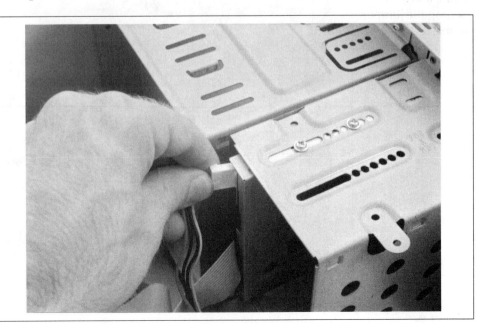

The 20 GB IDE Western Digital hard drive chosen is a low-cost drive that still delivers more capacity and performance than the best IDE drives of just a couple years ago. All the information required to install the drive is contained in the informative label on the cover.

Figure 6-48
Western Digital
Caviar 205AA

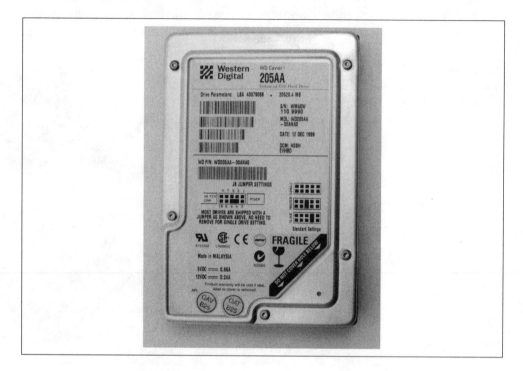

The first step to installing the hard drive into our system is to set the drive select jumper to "master". The CD drive will be set to "slave" and installed on the same ribbon cable.

Figure 6-49
Setting the jumper
to master

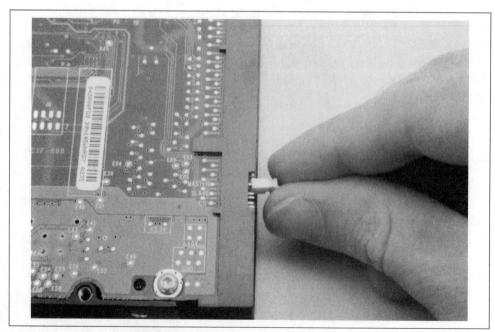

The hard drive is installed from the inside of the case in the 3.5" bay under the floppy drive. Line the drive up in a position where it can be secured with four screws. If the fit seems too tight as you try to slide the drive in, loosen the screws holding the floppy drive until it slides in easily. Do not put the drive in on an angle and try to straighten it in place.

Figure 6-50
Hard drive
installation

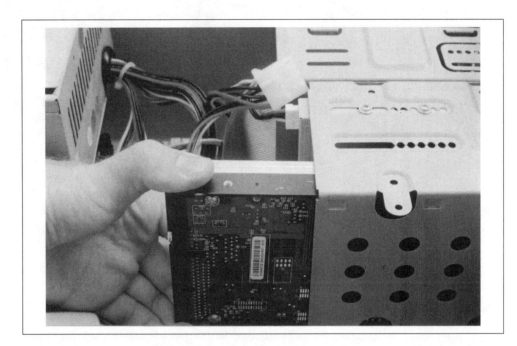

Secure the drive with four screws, two on each side, making sure the drive is level with the bottom of the cage. Retighten any screws you might have loosened in the floppy drive.

Figure 6-51
Securing the
hard drive

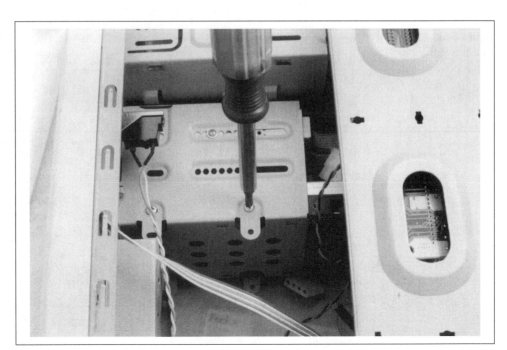

The hard drive ribbon cable is installed with the red wire in the connector keyed to pin 1. Most production hard drives orient the connector with pin 1 toward the power connector.

Figure 6-52
Installing the
IDE ribbon cable

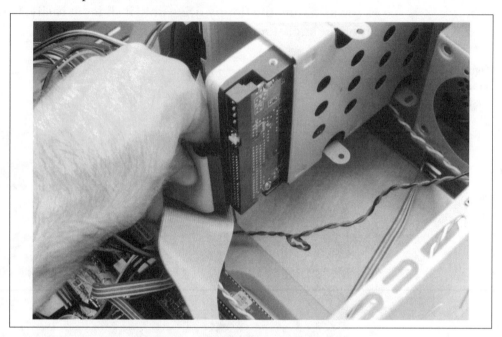

Hard drives are designed with a power connection socket that is keyed to the large connectors on the power supply leads by angling two corners of the socket so the connection can only be made one way. Take a good look at the connector and socket to identify the angled corners before mating the connection. The connector should push into the socket at least 1/4 inch, which often requires strong pressure.

Figure 6-53
Installing the hard
drive power lead

As an IDE device, our CD drive is equipped with a master/slave jumper, just like the hard drive. Because we will share an IDE cable between the two drives and the hard drive is set to "master", we set the CD drive to "slave" before installing the drive. Along with the IDE ribbon cable and the power lead, all CD drives have a connector for stereo sound that is active when you play a music CD in the drive. The thin cable might be labeled or keyed for keeping the left and right stereo channels straight, although it doesn't hurt anything if you get it backward. New drives usually sport a two pin connection for digital audio, as do most new sound cards or sound-enabled motherboards, but this connection is only required if you want to record digital music directly from CD, which is usually a violation of somebody's copyright.

Figure 6-54
Installing the slave jumper on the CD drive with cables (shown outside the case)

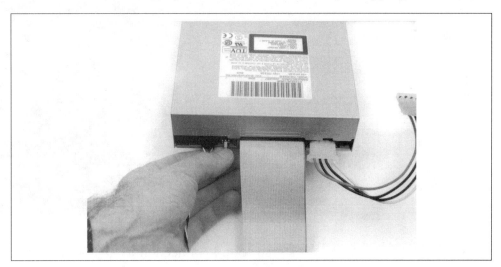

You can pop out the plastic cover for the top bay in the minitower case with your fingers. The drive can be installed in any of the 5.25" bays, but the top bay lacks the metal RF shield that covers the lower two bays, so it's most convenient to fill it first. The drive is then slid in from the front of the case. See the Athlon/Duron system for an example of mounting a CD drive with a rail assembly.

Figure 6-55
Sliding the CD drive into place

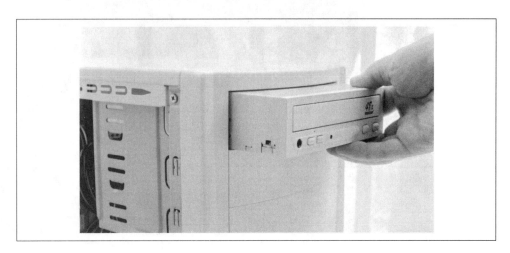

Secure the drive with four screws and connect the shared ribbon cable with the red wire on pin 1; then insert the keyed power lead. Connect the IDE ribbon cable to the primary IDE controller port on the motherboard. Check the motherboard manual for the orientation of pin 1 on the connector to match the red key wire in the ribbon, unless it is clearly marked on the board. Some motherboards ship with keyed IDE ribbon cables that have a special locking mechanism on the motherboard end, so the choice is made for you.

Figure 6-56
Connecting the CD drive power lead

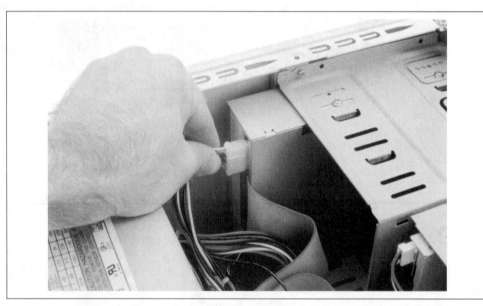

Make the stereo sound connection to the motherboard, which integrates the sound adapter functions. The motherboard offers two different CD sound connectors to accommodate both cable types currently in use.

Figure 6-57
Connect the CD stereo to motherboard

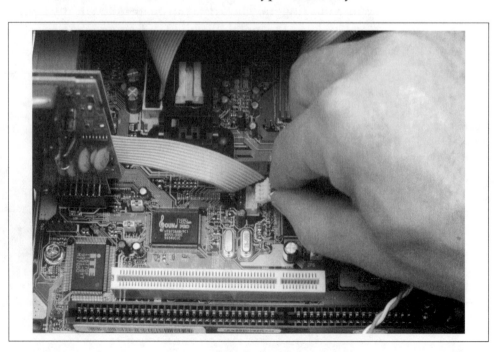

Step 8: Finishing Up and Closing the Case

The last step is normally to make the front panel connections to the motherboard. These include the case speaker, reset switch, power switch, power, and hard drive LEDs. You need to have the motherboard manual open for this procedure because the motherboard connector block is rarely labeled. If you find you have an LED that doesn't light when the build is complete, the connector for that LED is probably on backward.

Figure 6-58
Connecting the
front panel leads

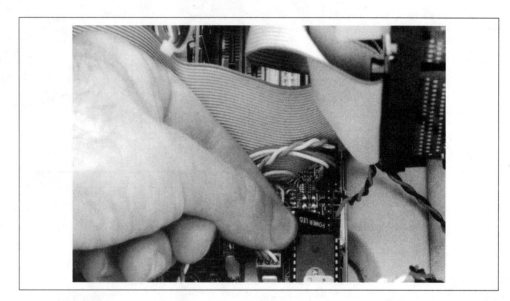

Lift the whole case off the table and gently shake it back and forth, listening for loose screws or other forgotten bits. Next, replace the bottom lid and screw it into place. If you have a clean work area and a monitor available, you might want to stand the case up and skip replacing the top lid until you turn the system on and see that all your connections were made correctly.

Figure 6-59
Closing the case

Check the voltage switch one more time and plug in the power cord. If the power supply is equipped with an override power switch as this supply is, turn that switch on. When working on this system in the future, the switch can be turned off, though I find it's safer to plug everything in through a switched power strip with a surge protector.

Figure 6-60
Plugging in
the power cord;
turning the
override switch on

Now connect the keyboard, mouse, monitor, phone line, and speakers if you have them. We show the keyboard and mouse connectors here. See the Athlon/Duron build for making more peripheral connections.

Figure 6-61
Connecting
the keyboard
and mouse

Step 9: CMOS Setup

The first time you power up your new PC, you will have to enter CMOS Setup to set the CPU and memory bus speed. This is usually accomplished by pressing the DEL key as soon as the first text appears on the screen, or by following onscreen instructions to enter CMOS, such as "Hit <F1> to enter Setup". The first task on entering CMOS Setup is to set the CPU speed. The Main Setup screen is navigated using the arrow keys. Go immediately to CPU Settings and press ENTER. See the Athlon/Duron system for a screen-by-screen tour of CMOS Setup.

Figure 6-62
Main Setup screen

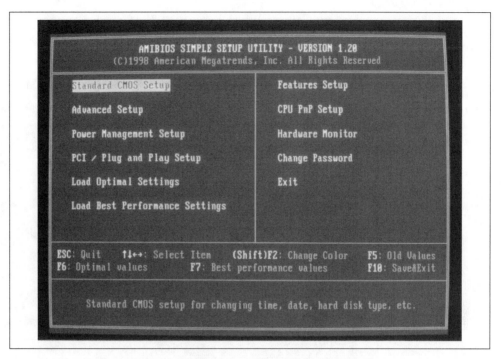

The system powers up for the first time at the lowest speed settings for universal compatibility. The Pentium III processor used here is a 500 MHz CPU with a 100 MHz front-side bus. First change the CPU Core Frequency, which fixes the bus speed from the default 66 MHz to 100 MHz by using the PAGE UP and PAGE DOWN or + and – keys as given in the onscreen instructions at the lower right. Next, change the multiplier until the CPU speed reaches 500 MHz, which requires a multiplier of 5X.

Figure 6-63
Setting the
Pentium III speed

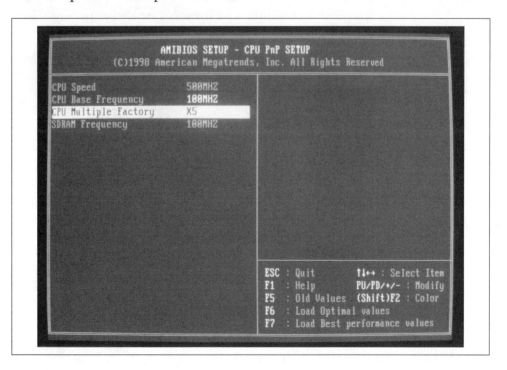

For our Celeron build, leave the CPU Core Frequency on the default 66 MHz and select the multiplier, 6X, which gives the 400 MHz CPU speed.

Figure 6-64
Setting the
Celeron speed

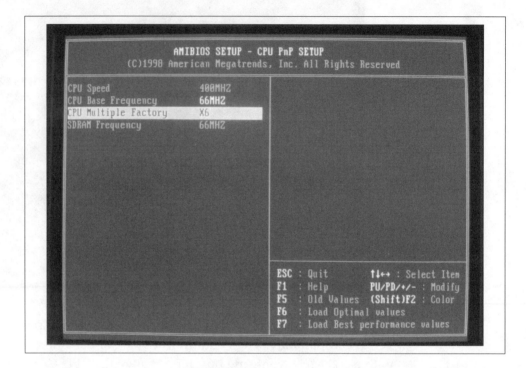

In either case, return to the Main Setup screen and go into Advanced where the speed of the SDRAM is set to 6 nS, because PC-133 memory is installed. Neither of the processors installed can take full advantage of the PC-133 module, designed to run on a 133 MHz front-side bus, but when there is no difference in module cost it makes no sense to buy the slower parts.

Figure 6-65
Setting the
SDRAM speed

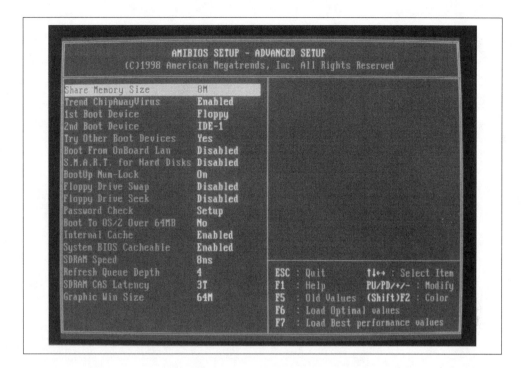

The final step is to exit CMOS and save the new settings. At this point the PC is completely built and the rest of the job is software installation. You do not need to set the drive types in CMOS Setup as with older PCs. A 1.44MB floppy drive for A: is the default and the IDE drives are automatically detected and configured. With a new motherboard such as this one, you don't even need to tell it to boot to the CD-ROM from which your operating system will be installed. The motherboard will check all the drives for a bootable disk without being told.

Chapter 7

Installing an Operating System

For the time being, the majority of PC builders will end up installing some version of Microsoft Windows on their PCs. Our example installation is Windows XP, the latest version of Windows available at press time. Windows XP is available in both business and home editions. We will install the home edition here. Other versions of Windows still in use include Windows Me, Windows 2000, and Windows 98 SE (Second Edition). The primary alternative to Windows is the freeware Linux operating system. Linux is *open source* software, meaning the actual software modules that make up the Linux operating system are available for programmers to modify. The Linux community is constantly posting enhancements and compatibility fixes on the Internet for free download. There are also several branded versions of Linux that come with extras such as phone support and installation CDs.

Since the advent of the bootable CD, all operating system installs have been rendered more or less the same. If the PC you are building is destined to be a server, you may want to have the IP (Internet Protocol) address handy as you install the software to save a step later. However, the only thing you really need to install an operating system is the serial number that ships with the CD. The trick comes after the operating system is installed and you start installing the drivers for specific hardware components, such as the motherboard and the video card. These components are sold with CDs, which often contain drivers for every bit of hardware the manufacturer sells, so just finding the correct driver on the CD can be frustrating. The best way I've found to install drivers from a CD is to skip by Windows requests for drivers by clicking Cancel and run the install software on the driver CD. We offer some solutions for failed operating system installs in Chapter 8.

The first Windows XP Setup screen offers three options: Setup Windows XP, Repair a Damaged Installation Using Repair Console, or Quit. The difference between a fresh setup and repairing a damaged installation is that if you have already installed XP and invested time in customizing, but have now lost some functionality, repairing should leave your customizations intact.

Figure 7-1
Initial Setup
screen

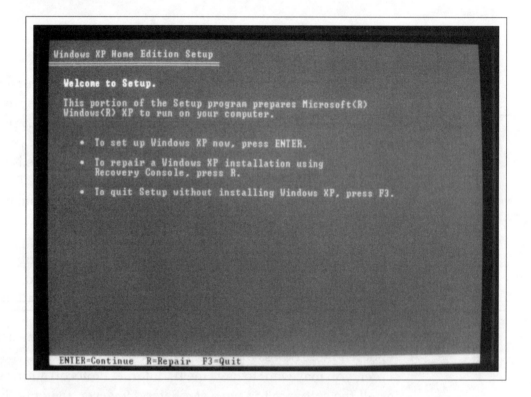

You have two choices when it comes to the Windows Licensing Agreement: you can agree to accept it or not. If you agree, the installation continues; if you don't, the installation is over. It's been a long, long time since I actually read the Licensing Agreement before accepting it.

Figure 7-2
Windows
Licensing
Agreement

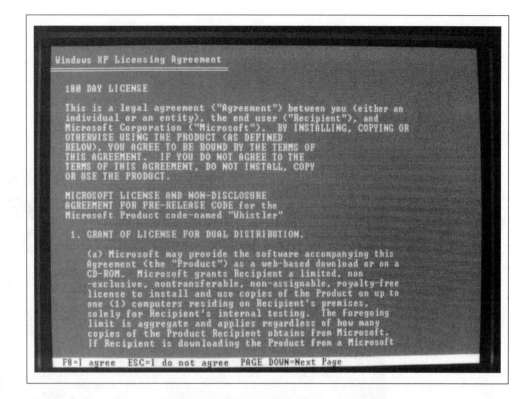

We don't have any reason to create multiple partitions on our hard drive, so we create a single partition using all the drive space. As soon as you press ENTER, the PC restarts and you are prompted to choose which partition to install XP on. Because you only have one partition, it's an easy choice.

Figure 7-3
Configuring the
hard drive space

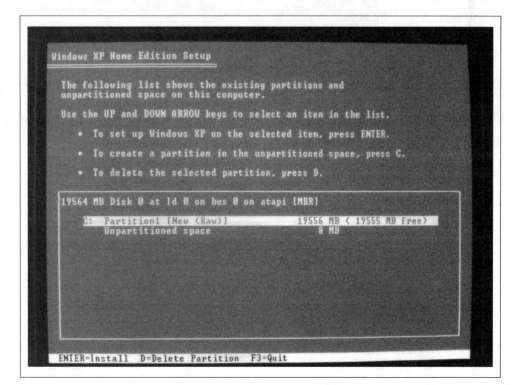

The next step is formatting the hard drive—laying down the basic structure for storing and retrieving files. The two choices are NTFS (New Technology File System) and FAT (File Allocation Table), with NTFS being the preferred choice. The quality of new hard drives is such that you can do a Quick Format, which lays down the structure without writing to every location on the drive.

Figure 7-4
Choosing the
format type

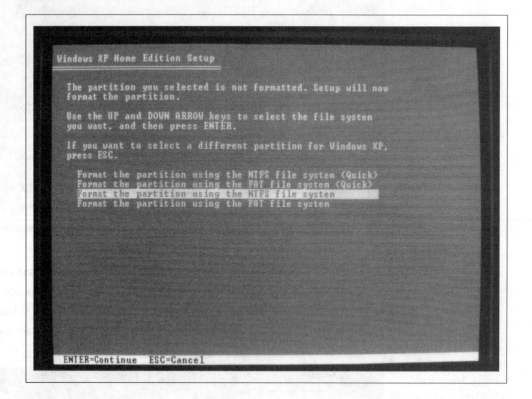

We did a traditional format, which took more than half an hour on a 20 GB hard drive. Microsoft does provide this exciting progress bar for your viewing pleasure. Immediately after the format, XP begins copying installation files to the hard drive, a process that is also accompanied by a progress bar.

Figure 7-5
Formatting the
hard drive

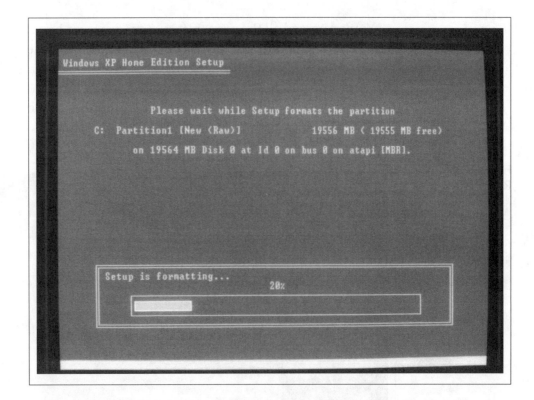

As soon as the copying process is complete, XP restarts the PC again. For some reason, Windows always give you a countdown to an automatic restart with the option to press any key and restart immediately. Once the PC restarts, it boots from the hard drive rather than from the CD.

Figure 7-6
Windows XP
splash screen

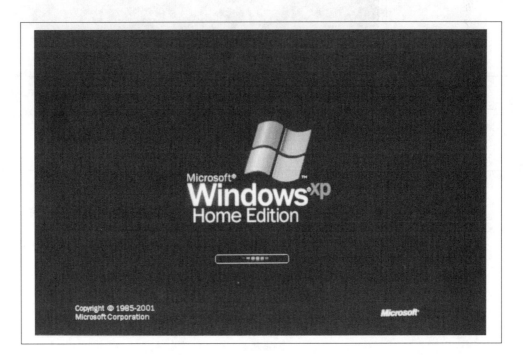

You've passed all the preparatory steps now and have arrived at actually installing the operating system. The first step is to choose regional and language options; later screens will include setting the date and time, networking preferences, keyboard and mouse types, and so forth. This is a common place for the installation to fail if there is a problem with reading the CD drive.

Figure 7-7
Regional settings

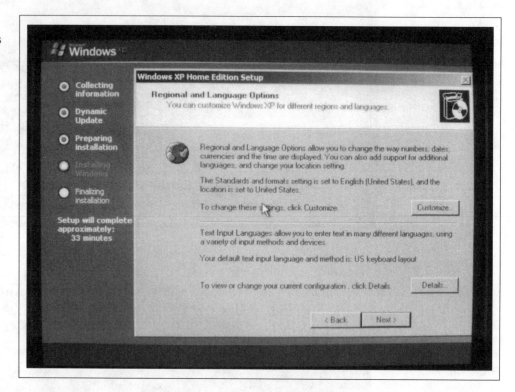

The next screen prompts you for your name (not the computer name) and the organization name. This is strictly registration information. You'll have a chance to configure computer name and networking workgroup or domain name later.

Figure 7-8
Registration
information

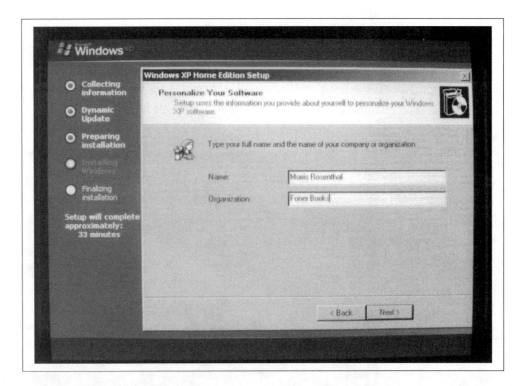

The product key is found on the envelope the install CD shipped in, although earlier and customized versions of Windows might ship with the serial number on the back of the installation booklet or on a separate license agreement. It's extremely easy to make a typing error entering the 25-character long code, in fact, I rarely get it right on the first go.

Figure 7-9
Entering the
serial number

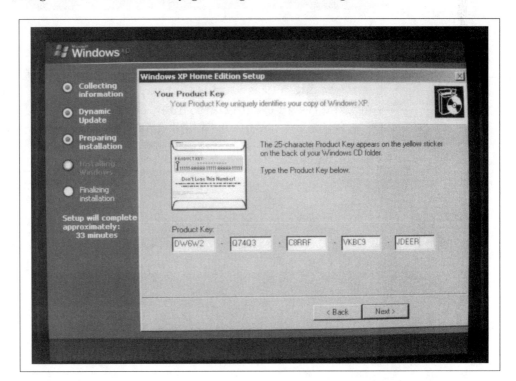

After XP leads you through a couple more screens, similar to Figure 7-7, it saves all these settings. The home edition of Windows XP is positioned as a home entertainment enhancement over earlier Windows versions, with integrated support for digital cameras and multimedia. It also sports another exciting progress bar on the bottom left of the screen.

Figure 7-10
Finalizing
Windows settings

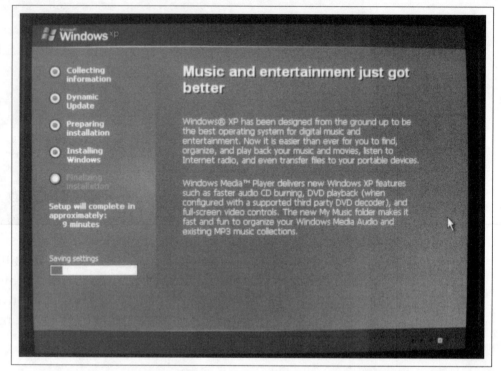

All Windows operating systems support multiple users who can be assigned passwords. The advantage of logging on to Windows with a username and a password is that any subsequent passwords you need to enter, such as for logging on to Internet sites, can be saved in a list. By entering that one password when you start Windows, all your other passwords will be remembered.

Figure 7-11
Adding user
names

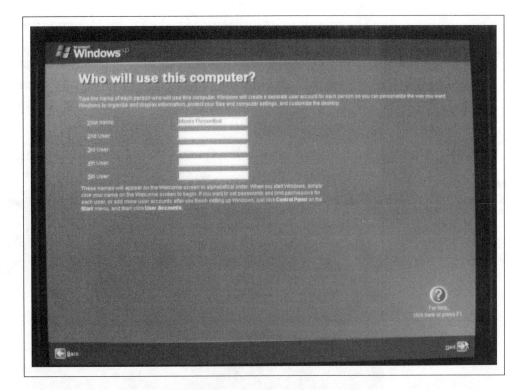

Windows XP has replaced the old blue sky and clouds of previous Windows versions with a pastoral scene, which still includes blue sky and clouds. The Start menu has also been reorganized with what is intended to be a more user-friendly interface, but to the majority of users who are familiar with older Windows versions, it's just window dressing.

Figure 7-12
The XP Start
menu

The most important feature for the PC builder and troubleshooter in any version of Windows is the Control Panel. The XP Control Panel is poorly organized for this purpose, but you can display the Classic Control Panel, which has looked the same since Windows 95. Within the Classic Control Panel, Device Manager, which is accessed through the System icon, is the place to go for hardware troubleshooting.

Figure 7-13
XP Control Panel

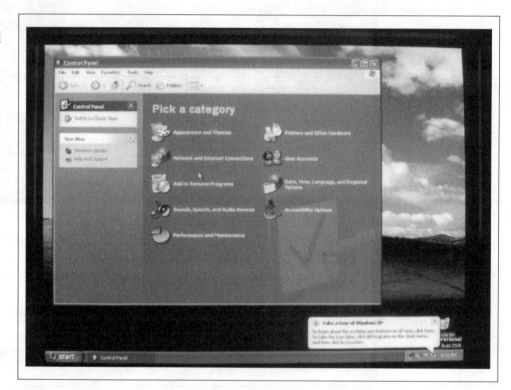

Chapter 8

Troubleshooting Checklists

The first step in troubleshooting your new PC is to double-check that you followed the assembly guidelines in Chapter 3. As stressed in that chapter, the most common problem with any new PC build is partially made or improper connections. Most of the troubleshooting procedures in this chapter require that the cover be removed from the PC and that some components be removed or reconnected. For this reason, it's best to plug in the PC through a switched power strip, so you can use the power strip switch to isolate the system from the electrical supply before every repair attempt.

Most people, even professional technicians, tend to get a little sloppy when troubleshooting, often accidentally introducing a new problem to replace the old. The main key to any type of troubleshooting is to go one step at a time. That way, when the original problem is corrected, you'll know exactly what did the trick, and if you create a new problem, you'll know what went wrong.

We will address five basic scenarios in this chapter, ranging from a stone dead system to a lack of functionality, such as a modem that won't connect. Although these procedures will uncover most assembly errors, there is often no way to isolate a dead component without having other known good parts to swap out. In the world of professional PC troubleshooting and repair, the "swap 'til you drop" strategy is still the most common troubleshooting technique employed. Swapping components requires no expensive diagnostics software or hardware and is usually the quickest way to isolate a problem. Another reason to steer clear of specialized diagnostics tools is that they are geared to identifying problems with subcomponents that can't be fixed anyway. Finding out exactly which address is bad in the system RAM or in the cache memory of a drive or motherboard is of little use when you'll have to replace the whole assembly anyway.

These troubleshooting procedures are for a newly built PC. If you have been using the PC for some time, for any new problem that arises you have to consider the possibility of a computer virus. One way to check whether you have a hardware problem or a virus problem at boot time is to boot from your original operating system CD. If you do contract a virus, there are many virus doctor programs you can buy with a reasonable certainty they will fix the problem, but you may need Internet access to download the latest virus inoculations from the software manufacturer's Web site.

In general, if you encounter a serious recurring software problem with your PC, and you have good backups of any important data, the most reliable fix is to wipe clean the hard drive by deleting the primary partition with the FDISK program and reinstall the software from scratch. Just be really sure you have the original CDs and serial numbers for all the software you use, in addition to good data backups, because once you FDISK, it's all gone. Before running FDISK, confirm that your operating system CD will boot!

Caution: We cannot reiterate enough times that you should disconnect power from the system before making any change inside the case; then reconnect after each change to check the result. If you smell a burnt electronics odor at any time, you have a blown component and should not attempt powering up again until it is found and replaced and the cause of the failure is determined.

Scenario 1: Stone Dead

You switch on your new system and there are no signs of life. The power supply fan doesn't turn, there are no sounds, no lights.

❑ Make sure the power cord is fully inserted into the power supply, the override switch on the back of the supply (if so equipped) is turned on, and the voltage switch is set correctly. Don't neglect to make sure the wall socket you are plugged into is live by unplugging the computer and plugging in a radio or lamp to check.

❑ Recheck the motherboard documentation for the proper connection of the leads from the front panel power switch. Don't settle for just looking at the switch connection to the motherboard; remove the lead, check that the terminal block matches the documentation, and then reconnect it. Undo the main power supply connection to the motherboard (this requires pressing in the clasp as you pull gently on the connector), inspect the connector for damage, and reconnect. On Pentium 4 systems make sure you have connected the additional 12V header.

❏ Search for shorted components by disconnecting the power cables and ribbon cables from the drives, one drive at a time, retrying power up after each drive is disconnected. Without reconnecting the drives, remove each adapter card (leave video for last) one at a time, retrying power up after each removal.

❏ Remove and reinstall memory DIMMs or RIMMs, inspecting for physical damage. Remove and reinstall the heatsink and CPU, double checking the CPU fan is connected to the proper terminal on the motherboard. Never attempt to power up the system without the heatsink installed.

❏ In extremely rare cases, the power switch on the front panel may be faulty. You can use a continuity checker or Ohm-meter to check the switch, or you can connect the front panel reset switch as a test.

❏ Remove the motherboard from the case and check for loose screws, extra standoffs, and anything else that could cause a short circuit to the motherboard circuitry. Reinstall the motherboard in the case and reinstall the video adapter, then try powering up.

If you still have no power, the problem is most likely a defective power supply or motherboard.

Scenario 2: Power Comes On; Screen Is Dead

You hear the power come on and the drives spinning up, but the screen remains blank.

❏ Make sure the monitor is plugged into a good power outlet by switching wall sockets with the power supply cord. If the power cord is not permanently attached to the monitor, make sure it is fully inserted in the socket on the back of the monitor. If your monitor is equipped with manual dials for brightness and contrast, make sure they are in the middle of their range.

❏ Remove the monitor connector from the video card and check that none of the pins in the shell are bent over. Note that some missing pins in the three-row high-density connector are normal.

❏ Remove and reseat the video adapter, making sure the hold-down screw doesn't cause the back end of the adapter to lift partially out of the connector.

❑ Check for a defective or conflicting adapter on the bus. Remove any other adapters installed, one by one, rechecking power after each. Don't forget to unplug the power supply, or turn off the power strip or override switch before each removal.

❑ Double-check the motherboard documentation for overlooked CPU selection switches or jumpers settings. Depending on the motherboard used, CPU selection might be automatic. Don't take the manual at its word that the default settings are set; check the actual switch and jumper positions on the motherboard.

❑ Double-check that CPU and memory modules are seated properly, particularly slot-type CPUs, which can take a good deal of pressure to mate correctly with the motherboard.

If you still have no live screen, the problem is likely defective hardware. Make sure the case speaker is properly connected to the motherboard as per the motherboard documentation. If you hear a series of beeps, note the number and sequence, as they will pinpoint the defective component. The motherboard documentation or manufacturer Web site should give the codes, although the most likely candidate for beeps on a dead screen is the video adapter. If no beeps sound, the most likely candidates are a dead monitor (easily checked by connecting it to another system), a defective motherboard, or a defective power supply. In some instances, you may have bad RAM or a bad video adapter but still not hear any beep codes.

Scenario 3: Screen Comes On; No Boot

You get text appearing onscreen, but the PC either won't try to boot or locks up in the process.

❑ No onscreen messages indicating boot failure.

❑ Enter CMOS Setup by following onscreen instructions (usually by pressing the DEL or F1 key) after power up. Select the CMOS option to Restore Default Settings or similarly phrased option, save, and reboot. *Note:* If you cannot access Setup, double-check that the keyboard and mouse connectors aren't interchanged. If you still can't access Setup, disconnect power and remove all adapters except the video and disconnect the drives. If you still can't access Setup, you have some defective hardware, most likely the motherboard, although it could still be the RAM or CPU. These core components should always be bought from the same source to simplify return issues.

❏ If there are still no messages indicating boot failure, enter CMOS Setup again and make sure the CPU speed setting, bus clock frequency, and IDE interface speed don't exceed your components ratings.

❏ If the system hangs at Verifying DMI Data Pool, it is usually a motherboard or IDE device problem. If you have an option to enable Reset Configuration Data, use it. Disconnect your IDE cables from the motherboard and see if you can get as far as a Drive Failure or No Boot Device message. If not, the motherboard will probably need replacing, although you can try discharging the onboard battery first by using the jumper setting in the motherboard manual for disabling a forgotten password.

❏ Missing operating system or no boot device message.

❏ Check that the IDE cables are connected to the drives and motherboard properly by removing and reinstalling them. Make sure the power connectors to all the drives are properly installed. Make sure the master/slave jumpers for the drives are installed properly.

❏ If the system tries to boot a CD and fails, it may just be bad timing. Strangely enough, some high-speed CD drives take so long to get up to speed that the BIOS (motherboard logic) gives up on them before they get there. If the screen displays a message such as "Insert CD and hit any key when ready," eject the CD tray; then push it back in, but wait until you hear the drive spin up before pressing a key to continue. It might take a few efforts to get this right if it's going to work.

❏ Check that the operating system CD is readable in another system, and don't try using pirated operating system software on home recorded CDs.

❏ Enter CMOS Setup and rearrange the boot sequence so that the CD-ROM or the IDE channel to which it is connected is selected as the first boot device. This shouldn't be necessary, but it will help if a previous attempt to install the operating system failed, leaving the hard drive appearing bootable to the motherboard.

❏ Simplify the system by removing any additional drives so all you have left are a "master" hard drive on the primary IDE channel and a "master" CD on the secondary IDE channel. If it doesn't work, as a final check try both drives on the primary controller with the CD as the "slave."

Scenario 4: Boots; Locks Up During or After OS Install

Everything appears to be working fine, right up through formatting the hard drive. But, at some point during the operating system installation or immediately after, the PC locks up.

❑ First check with your parts vendor or operating system manufacturer for known compatibility issues. Also be aware that some CDRs and combination drives have problems with operating system install, which usually manifests itself as a "read error."

❑ Unplug the power and remove all adapters except the video adapter. Install the operating system. Next install the motherboard drivers from the CD that shipped with the motherboard and the video adapter driver from its own CD. Install any other adapters one at a time, reconnect power and reboot, allowing the operating system to deal with them individually.

❑ Make sure you are using the approved cabling for any high-performance parts such as 80-conductor ribbon cables with Ultra 66 or Ultra 100 hard drives, because communication breakdowns at high speeds are likely to show up under the load of operating system installation.

❑ In some rare cases, operating system installation can fail repeatedly because a borderline component is suffering a heat-related failure as the system warms up. This is extremely difficult to troubleshoot without parts to swap out, and if you bring the parts back to the point of purchase, it might be hard to convince the vendor that the problem isn't in your imagination. Make sure the CPU heatsink is properly installed, the heatsink fan is working, and you aren't building the system in a hot attic in the summer. Go through the steps related to CMOS Setup in scenario 3 and document all the troubleshooting steps you go through for the vendor. Try reinstalling the operating system several times with no adapter other than video before concluding that you have a hardware failure.

Scenario 5: Boots and Runs

If your operating system installation goes smoothly but you have trouble accessing a particular device, the problem is as likely to be software as hardware. Extensive software troubleshooting is outside the scope of this book, but we will mention some of the key points you can check in Windows operating systems.

Floppy Drive

❏ If the activity light on the front of the floppy drive stays lit all the time, the ribbon cable on the drive or motherboard is probably backward.

❏ If the drive is not detected properly by CMOS Setup or recognized by the operating system, either the ribbon cable or power cord is partially or improperly connected (see Chapter 3), or the drive or a cable is bad. Replace the ribbon cable and try another power supply lead if one is available.

❏ For any problems reading or writing specific floppy disks, either the disk is bad or the drive that wrote the disk is incompatible with the drive trying to read it due to head alignment issues. Both of these problems are super-common and I've seen a 30 percent failure rate on brand-new "100 percent certified" floppy disks.

Hard Drive

❏ Any message indicating a hard drive read or write failure is a hardware error. Try replacing the ribbon cable, making sure you use the newer 80-conductor type.

❏ Isolate the hard drive on its own IDE channel, moving any other drives to the secondary channel on their own cable or temporarily disconnecting them.

❏ If the hard drive is excessively noisy or makes a continual clunking sound, it has suffered internal damage and odds are even an expensive data recovery outfit won't be able to help.

❏ If the errors persist, either the drive or IDE controller is bad. If you can disable the motherboard IDE controller in CMOS (both channels), you can try substituting an inexpensive PCI IDE controller before giving up on the motherboard. You can also try lowering the transfer speed in CMOS Setup, but if the problem goes away, you are sacrificing performance.

CD or DVD Drive

❏ If the drive has trouble reading a particular disc, try wiping off any fingerprints with a clean flannel shirt. Note rewriteable discs written in CDRs and DVDRs are often unreadable in other drives.

❏ For continual read errors, try all the steps for hard drive troubleshooting: new IDE cable, isolation, and swapping IDE controller. CD and DVD drives are far less standardized than hard drives, so isolating them on their own controller will often fix the problem.

❏ If you can't play music CDs even though your speakers work with other computer sounds, the thin audio cable from the sound card (or motherboard with integrated sound) to the four-pin connector on the back of the drive is improperly installed or missing.

❏ If you record music CDs on your PC and they won't play in your stereo, make sure you are using CDR blanks, not CDRW.

❏ If you have a CDR or DVDR and your write sessions often fail, try recording at a lower speed and make sure you are using media certified for at least the speed at which you are recording.

Modem

❏ Check that the phone line from the wall goes into the modem jack labeled "line." Plug a regular handset into the modem jack labeled phone. If you don't hear a dial tone, either the modem or the phone line is dead.

❏ In Windows, go to Start | Settings | Control Panel | Modems | Diagnostics | More Info. If your modem doesn't show up in Windows, power down and try removing all the other adapters except the video card from the PC before rebooting. If Windows still doesn't find your modem, try it in a different motherboard slot. If Windows still can't find the modem, it is probably defective or incompatible.

❏ If you hear the modem dial but the only thing that happens is that after a while the operator picks up, you are probably dialing tone on a pulse system.

❏ If you never get connect speeds over 33K, contact your Internet service provider with your modem information.

❏ If you connect between 33K and 53K but with inconsistent speed and frequent disconnects, you probably have aging or overloaded local phone infrastructure. Try another phone jack in your house in case it is a just a poorly wired outlet. Try using the modem outside of business hours, particularly morning and after school, when traffic is heaviest.

❏ Don't daisy chain too many phone devices, such as fax to computer to computer. The weakest link in the telephone infrastructure is the RJ-11 jack on the ends of the short phone cords you connect from device to device.

Sound Card

❏ Check Windows Device Manager to see whether there are any conflicts and be sure the sound card drivers are installed. Device Manager can be invoked either through Start | Settings | Control Panel | System or by *right-clicking* (right-hand mouse button) My Computer and choosing Properties. If Windows didn't recognize the sound card, try powering down and removing the other adapters, except the video card, from the PC before rebooting. If Windows still doesn't find your sound card, try it in a different motherboard slot. If it still can't find the sound card, it probably is defective or incompatible.

❏ Make sure your speakers are plugged into the correct jack on the sound card, because the little pictures can be deceptively similar. The speaker jack usually is the one right above the game port. Make sure speakers with an external power source are plugged in and turned on, and that the volume dial isn't off.

❏ If you have been using your PC for a while and then lose all sound, the most common reason is the "mute" box being mysteriously checked in one of the innumerable mixer panels that install with sound card software. Happy hunting!

Network

❏ If the network adapter doesn't appear in Device Manager, try powering down and removing the other adapters, except the video card, from the PC before rebooting. If Windows still doesn't find your network adapter, try it in a different motherboard slot. If it still can't find the adapter, it probably is defective or incompatible.

❏ If the card looks healthy in Device Manager but you can't connect to your local network, check all the software protocols and identification settings in Start | Settings | Control Panel | Network. For home networks, getting the Workgroup name wrong is the most common error.

❏ If you are sure you have all your software settings right by comparing them line for line with another PC on the network, you have a cabling problem. Most small networks are wired for 10/100 BaseT, but the cables are often built incorrectly. 10BaseT and 100BaseTX use four conductors in two pairs in an RJ-45 connector, 1&2 and 3&6. Some other standards use all eight wires in four pairs, but the important point in every case is that 3 and 6 must utilize a color-coded pair, something many cable makers still neglect.

Video

❑ If the screen seems jumpy, particularly from a distance, it could be the monitor. Another possibility is interference from electrical equipment such as an external transformer for speakers or other devices resting near the back of the monitor. In industrial environments, electrical wiring in walls carrying high currents can cause wavy interference.

❑ If you look at the screen out of the corner of your eye and it seems to flash near the edges or bottom, the vertical refresh frequency is probably too low. You can try a lower screen resolution or change video modes if the video card software gives you that option.

❑ If you are missing a primary color, check the 15-pin video connector to see whether any of the pins are bent over. If not, you have probably lost one of the electron guns in the monitor, requiring warranty repair.

Printers, Scanners, and Other External Peripherals

❑ If your printer or other external device can't be detected, make sure you are using a new, approved cable for connecting the device and that it is plugged in and powered on. Older parallel cables often fail with new printers even though the connectors match. Many new printers have no power switch, as they are always on and waiting for jobs in a low power mode when plugged in.

❑ Check in CMOS Setup that you have selected the proper port protocol to work with the device. Some printers, scanners, and external drives require you to set the port to ECP (Extended Capability Port) or EPP (Enhanced Parallel Port) for two-way communications and increased speed. The default setting for the printer port in Setup is usually Normal, which doesn't support any of these advanced functions.

❑ If the device is detected but times out, make sure you have followed the unpacking and initial setup instructions, such as unlocking a scanner or properly installing the toner and paper in a printer.

❑ Try using a single power strip to power your PC and all the peripherals to obtain a common ground. You might have a ground loop where current is actually present on the grounds of the signal cables due to the devices being plugged into different outlets in a room. Sometimes an outlet has a compromised ground, which leaves the PC and the peripheral grounds at different potentials. This can create a current flow that results in unpredictable operation.

Index

INTERNATIONAL CONTACT INFORMATION

AUSTRALIA
McGraw-Hill Book Company Australia Pty. Ltd.
TEL +61-2-9417-9899
FAX +61-2-9417-5687
http://www.mcgraw-hill.com.au
books-it_sydney@mcgraw-hill.com

CANADA
McGraw-Hill Ryerson Ltd.
TEL +905-430-5000
FAX +905-430-5020
http://www.mcgrawhill.ca

**GREECE, MIDDLE EAST,
NORTHERN AFRICA**
McGraw-Hill Hellas
TEL +30-1-656-0990-3-4
FAX +30-1-654-5525

MEXICO (Also serving Latin America)
McGraw-Hill Interamericana Editores S.A. de C.V.
TEL +525-117-1583
FAX +525-117-1589
http://www.mcgraw-hill.com.mx
fernando_castellanos@mcgraw-hill.com

SINGAPORE (Serving Asia)
McGraw-Hill Book Company
TEL +65-863-1580
FAX +65-862-3354
http://www.mcgraw-hill.com.sg
mghasia@mcgraw-hill.com

SOUTH AFRICA
McGraw-Hill South Africa
TEL +27-11-622-7512
FAX +27-11-622-9045
robyn_swanepoel@mcgraw-hill.com

**UNITED KINGDOM & EUROPE
(Excluding Southern Europe)**
McGraw-Hill Education Europe
TEL +44-1-628-502500
FAX +44-1-628-770224
http://www.mcgraw-hill.co.uk
computing_neurope@mcgraw-hill.com

ALL OTHER INQUIRIES Contact:
Osborne/McGraw-Hill
TEL +1-510-549-6600
FAX +1-510-883-7600
http://www.osborne.com
omg_international@mcgraw-hill.com